It's All in How You Tell It

Preaching First-Person Expository Messages

Haddon W. Robinson
Torrey W. Robinson

Published by Baker Books
a division of Baker Publishing Group
P.O. Box 6287, Grand Rapids, MI 49516-6287
www.bakerbooks.com

Fourth printing, August 2006

Printed in the United States of America

Library of Congress Cataloging-in-Publication Data
Robinson, Torrey W., 1957–
It's all in how you tell it : preaching first-person expository messages / Torrey W. Robinson and Haddon W. Robinson
p. cm.
Includes bibliographical references.
ISBN 10: 0-8010-9150-0 (pbk.)
ISBN 978-0-8010-9150-6 (pbk.)
1. Preaching. I. Robinson, Haddon W. II. Title.
BV4211.3 .R595 2003
251—dc21 2002014960

To Carey and Carl:

Almost a hundred and fifty years ago, in Northern Ireland, your great-great grandfather staggered home drunk past a church where they were singing an old hymn:

> There is life for a look at the crucified one.
> There is life at this moment for thee.
> Look sinner look unto him and be saved,
> Unto him who died on the tree.
> Look, look, look and live
> To him who died on the tree.

Hearing the words of that hymn, your great-great-grandpa surrendered his life to Christ and became a lay preacher. All his children became Christians. By God's grace, that story, that faith was passed on to your great-grandfather, to your grandfather, and then to your father. Now that story has become your story.

It is our prayer that your children and your grandchildren may know the truth of that story as they see it lived out in you.

Contents

Key Terms

The following terms are important to the discussion of first-person preaching and will be employed in this book:

Anachronisms: Jargon or references that are out of their proper historical time. For example, Joseph wore sandals, not shoes. He was a slave, not an employee, in Potiphar's house.

Blocking: Assigning a location on the stage to the character or characters in each scene.

Characterization: The way the author or narrator describes, contrasts, parallels, and depicts the words and actions of the characters in the narrative.

Chronological Development: A story constructed chronologically, that is, one event following another as it happened in time.

Deduction: Reasoning from the general to the specific. Most sermons of the last fifty years in the Western world have tended to follow a deductive pattern. They usually start with a summary point and move from this general assertion to the specific details or subpoints of the sermon.

Dramatic Monologue: A sermon preached from the viewpoint of an eyewitness to an event.

Exposition: Preaching which "confronts the hearers with an accurate interpretation of the biblical revelation and its present meaning for their lives."[1]

First-Person Sermon: (same as dramatic monologue)

First-Person Expository Sermon: An expository sermon preached from a first-person perspective. In other words, this preaching form is based on an accurate interpretation of the Scripture and applies its meaning to the hearers. It does this through the retelling of the scriptural account from the vantage point of a character who was part of the story.

Flashback: An interruption in the continuity of a story that relays an earlier episode.

Genre: In reference to literature, it is the specific type or classification of the literary work such as prose, poetry, or narrative.

Hermeneutically Inconsequential: In a few biblical texts (such as the parables of Jesus), the historicity and identity of the characters are not essential to the interpretation and preaching of the narrative.

Hermeneutically Indispensable: In most narrative biblical texts, the historicity and identity of the character or characters were assumed by the biblical writer and are essential to the interpretation and preaching of the narrative.

Historical Narrative: A nonfiction story.

Homiletics: The preparation and delivery of sermons.

Induction: Reasoning from the specific to the general. Stories are inductive, moving from specific actions and events to a general moral or lesson.

Narrative: A story, either fiction or nonfiction.

Narrative Literature: The literary genre also known as story.

Psychological Development: A narrative constructed or relayed by a thought sequence rather than chronologically. The unfolding of the story is not based on a steady progression in time. Instead, the story develops logically or according to another expected flow of thought.

Stance: In first-person preaching, stance describes the perspective of the character in relation to the twenty-first-century audience. For example, does the character know the audience? Is the character familiar with his or her culture? Is the audience listening to the character on the ancient scene, or is the character imaginatively transported into the twenty-first century?

Third-Person Narrative: A story communicated by a narrator who is not part of the story being told. For example, in his Gospel, Luke gives a third-person narrative account of the life of Jesus.

1

From Egg Rolls to Stealth Bombers

The pastor slumped down in his seat opposite me in the restaurant and played with his water glass. Then he made a comment that sounded like a confession: "I am bored, very bored, with my own preaching." He was an effective leader of the largest church in a half-gallon town in the Midwest. He administered a staff of seven that oversaw a variety of ministries within the congregation and the community. But when it came to preaching, he gave himself low marks. He summed up his pulpit work in the words of a member of his church who described his sermons as a "tad or two above average."

What surprised me, though, was how he put it. He wasn't saying, "I am afraid that I am boring my congregation." He was admitting something even more deadening: "I am boring myself with my own preaching."

He wasn't talking about the grinding regularity of producing a new sermon each week. He carved out at least twelve hours a week from his demanding schedule for sermon preparation, and he enjoyed working in the biblical text. He studied, and he had something important to say. He wasn't bored with the Bible; he was bored with himself. His problem wasn't content; it was creativity. No matter where he was in the Scriptures, no matter what genre of literature he was preaching, one size fit all. He was sick of it.

His sermons resembled rows and rows of Chinese egg rolls. They were nourishing enough, but they all looked the same. He had used the same mold for over twenty years with little variety except for the subject matter. His sermons from the Psalms differed little from those out of Revelation. It was this unrelenting sameness that prompted him to say, "I am bored, very bored, with my own preaching."

He had good reason to be concerned. Boredom is like anthrax. It can kill. More people have been bored out of the Christian faith than have been reasoned out of it. Dull, insipid sermons not only cause drooping eyes and nodding heads, they destroy life and hope. What greater damage can we do to people's faith than to make them feel like God and Jesus Christ and the Bible are as boring as the want ads in the Sunday paper? Boredom can dull the life of the listener in the pew, but in this case it had infected the preacher.

He had learned how to hammer sermons together in seminary. The form he had been taught served him well in organizing his thoughts, but it was the only form he knew. Find a key word, arrange the points around that word, if possible alliterate them, review the points at the conclusion, toss in some application, and pray. The only variety was the central word he used to hold his sermons together. He had done this forty-five weeks a year for twenty years. Egg rolls every Sunday. No wonder he was bored.

He needed to understand that there are other ways to preach. There is no such entity as "the best sermon form." Sermons can take various forms, but no preaching form came down from heaven. The most common form sermons have taken through the centuries came from the Greeks and Romans. Many early preachers were educated as public speakers in the Roman schools. In their schooling, rhetoric was as important as writing. Educated people learned the communication theories of Aristotle, Cicero, and Quintilian, and they studied the speeches of gifted orators. Brilliant speakers were celebrities in ancient culture as much as actors and musicians are in ours, and students were encouraged to imitate them. So it isn't at all surprising that early church leaders injected secular theory about speechmaking into the Christian faith.

Basically, the method was deductive. It presented, defended, and won approval for a proposition. This classical approach had some strength. It probably led to the three-point sermon. The ancient orators asked and answered three questions: "What is it?" "Why would I want it?" and "How do I get it?" Later these questions were flattened to the formula "tell them what you're going to tell them, tell them, then tell them what you told them." The pastor had learned a modern variation of this form, and it was all he knew. Somehow he felt preaching in this form was the only way to be faithful to the Bible. Although it aided clarity, it stifled suspense. The method does have a venerable past, but it isn't eternal. It wasn't carried to earth by the angels.

The Scriptures provide no single form that Christian sermons must take. Indeed, the biblical authors used a myriad of different methods. They told stories and parables, composed psalms and recounted visions, reported history and wrote letters—all forms borrowed from their cultures and used to communicate what they had to say. No single sermon form has God's stamp of approval on it saying "Accept no substitutes." There are many different ways to communicate God's truth. Any minister reluctant to acknowledge this fact will speak with boring predictability.

Sermons can take various forms in the service of the Word. Many effective preachers today use an inductive development. This approach recognizes that the place of the preacher in our society has changed. In the recent past, ministers were regarded as authorities. In some communities the minister was the most educated person in town. He went into his study during the week to search the Bible for a message and would appear on Sunday to tell his congregation what he had discovered. The people listened because they believed the preacher was fully qualified to tell them what to think and how to live. That kind of influence has gone the way of running boards on automobiles. Today's culture rarely grants them authority, except perhaps what it grants to a justice of the peace to officiate at weddings.

Preachers have only the authority they can win for their message. If preachers understand that they occupy an office with only a sliver of respect, they will more often develop sermons inductively. In the first century the apostles weren't held in high regard by their antagonistic society, and that explains why the sermons reported in Acts were usually developed in an inductive manner. Inductive sermons, like inductive Bible studies, are structured so that the hearers discover the message for themselves. For those who believe that the Bible is self-authenticating and possesses its own power, this form can have great advantages today. The dynamic for the sermon lies less with the preacher and more with the Scriptures themselves. The preacher still studies, of course, but the message unfolds a part at a time so that listeners arrive at the conclusion with the pastor. Inductive sermons resemble a lively conversation more than a lecture.

One particular form of the inductive method is to tell a story. Stories have solid scriptural warrant. The writers of the Bible relied on stories to communicate their messages. The authors of many Old Testament books were accomplished storytellers, and they were also theologians. They used their stories to point people to God. The narratives in the Bible are not simply tales to tell children before they get tucked into bed at night; they are superbly crafted theology. Yet, in spite of the biblical witness to the power of stories, ministers sometimes feel they are "dumbing down" the truth if they use a narrative approach in their preaching. They simply won't believe that a story—even a biblical story—can carry the load.

When Jesus preached, he told stories. Perhaps it is because he was a storyteller that we don't think of Jesus as a theologian. Theologians are left-brained scholars telling people about God in propositions as vague and removed from life as mathematical formulas. In the Apostles' Creed, Jesus' entire teaching ministry is dismissed with a period or semicolon: "He was born of the Virgin Mary; suffered under Pontius Pilate." After all, who can rank anyone as a serious thinker who told tales about wandering sheep, lost grocery money, a runaway son, and a doting father, about invitations to a party that guests welcomed like a letter from the tax collector, or about a crazy grape grower who invented a ridiculous wage policy? Yet, these stories worked. Ordinary people responded to Jesus' parables with such interest that they walked miles to be in his audience. His enemies felt the point of those stories so painfully that they wiped him out. Stories are inductive; they resemble stealth bombers slipping in under people's defenses to deliver their load.

One of the best ways to develop a story is to use the first person, to climb inside the story and tell it from the perspective of one of the characters. Using a first-person point of view changes the angle and provides freshness and insight into what at first might seem pretty familiar stuff. Suppose you got inside the account of the temptation of Eve and Adam and changed the angle. How would Eve have explained what happened that afternoon? Or look at the incident from the tempter's angle; how would the serpent have justified his damning of the race? What was God's angle as he watched the couple under the attack of the Evil One? Why did he stand by and do nothing? Or suppose Adam looked back on the debacle fifty years later; how would he have talked about it? In using first-person narrative, you don't change the text, but you can change the angle.

In the case study Jesus told about a mugging on the Jericho highway, how would the different characters involved in the assault have answered the question, "Who is my neighbor?" How would the poor wretch who was robbed and left for dead have answered it? How about the priest who knew all about loving his neighbor as a theological abstraction but didn't recognize his neighbor lying beside the road in a pool of blood? When that pious traveler got home that evening and recounted to his wife what he had witnessed, how would he have justified himself? Would the couple then have bowed their heads to thank God that the bandits had not attacked him? Or get inside the head of the Samaritan who went out of his way to render assistance. He had the least to gain and the most to lose. Why did he bother to get involved in something that really wasn't his business? Tell that familiar parable from a fresh angle, and it can be as up-to-date as a rape victim left for dead in the neighborhood where you live.

Crafting a first-person sermon uses all of the analytical skills you have mastered in studying the biblical material, but it requires more. It calls on you to use your imagination as an interpretive tool. It is through imagination that the characters in the Bible cease being cardboard characters and jump from the page with life and power. In the following pages, we have tried to describe how you go about preparing and preaching a first-person expository sermon. If you can preach the Bible, you can preach this sermon form. You don't need to be an actor or even have superlative skills as a storyteller. You simply have to be willing to use both your right brain and your left brain in your study and then let the biblical characters speak for themselves. Try it once. You have nothing to lose but your boredom, and you have much to gain in presenting biblical truth in a fresh new way.

But we don't expect you to take our word for it. Listen to what preachers and teachers have to say about their experience preaching first-person expository sermons:

> "Being somewhat shy and inhibited, I would not have prepared a first-person sermon had one not been assigned by Dr. Robinson in one of his courses, and I would not have completed the assignment had it not been for the encouragement and help provided by Torrey. The resulting sermon on Daniel 4 turned out to be the most effective communication experience I have had in my ten years of teaching and preaching. It was the closest I have been to the congregation during a sermon and the most responsive they have been to a sermon. I would encourage all pastors . . . [to] add first-person sermons to their repertoire."
>
> —Daniel Hopkins, Grace Bible Church, Lorton, Virginia

> "Perhaps the greatest value of preaching in the first person is the effect that the process has on me. It forces me, as the preacher, to live in the world of the text . . . experiencing and understanding the meaning of the passage in a clear and powerful way."
>
> —Jody Bowser, The Chapel, Akron, Ohio

> "I was never involved in drama or theater as a youth but always wanted to try more expressive forms of communication than mere lecture. Using first-person narrative sermons in the pulpit has blossomed all sorts of creativity in the way I present material. In addition, it has freed up my mannerism and gesture such that all my other sermons tend to come across with more expression."
>
> —Brad Smith, Door Creek Church, Madison, Wisconsin

> "In my long years of teaching the process of preaching first-person sermons at Dallas Seminary, I have been impressed with the impact such preaching has had on the students' overall preaching effectiveness. Preachers who go through the process of devel-

oping, writing, and preaching first-person sermons will find their preaching ability significantly improved."

—John Reed, Dallas Theological Seminary, Dallas, Texas

"My first-person narrative sermon as Philemon brought the teaching of this letter from cold, hard facts leading to the 'so what' response, to a vivid, clear, fresh, and exciting look at a man struggling to forgive. The congregation's response was 'Wow, that was the best sermon you ever preached! When will you do it again?'"

—Ray DeLaurier, Pine Mountain Christian Community Church, Pine Mountain, California

"[After] one recent message on the centurion at the cross, I had people [in my congregation] speak about the impact of that message for months. One said to me, 'I never understood the cross until today.'"

—Jack DeVries, Bethel Christian Reformed Church, Listowel, Ontario, Canada

"Never in twenty-five years of ministry have I been so frightened at the prospect of preaching as I was the Sunday night I delivered my first narrative sermon. . . . To my eternal surprise, the congregation loved the experience, clearly understood the biblical message, and still talk about it a year later. Few of my sermons in twenty-five years of ministry have lived so long!"

—Don Denyes, South Church, Lansing, Michigan

"I loved learning to do first-person . . . sermons. I found it easy yet powerful, for the stories stayed in the listeners' minds."

—Beulah Wood, Faculty of South Asia Institute of Advanced Christian Studies, Bangalore, India

"I was hesitant to try first-person narrative preaching in my traditional church which often resists change. However, I noticed that my audience was riveted to my first attempt at a first-person narrative sermon. One listener said, 'I feel as if I had been sucked into the sermon with a vacuum.' My church has asked me to do a series of first-person narrative sermons during Lent."

—Ed Crotty, St. Thomas Lutheran Church, ELCA, Charlotte, North Carolina

"The first time I used first-person narrative was an experience of freedom. It loosed me from the confines of the pulpit and unlocked the biblical message for our congregation."

—Garth Williams, Union Street Baptist, St. Stephen, New Brunswick, Canada

"The congregation was a bit shocked for the first minute or so when I came out on stage dressed like Samson—long hair, blackened eyes, etc. I established who I was and that God had sent me back to earth to warn them of the results of a lust-filled life as I had lived it. The Spirit worked powerfully in a very quiet auditorium. There were conversations about it in the dorms for months afterward, not to mention numerous individuals who spoke personally with me up to a year later. The Holy Spirit used the first-person narrative form to slip the message past the defenses of the audience."

—Preston Busch, Briercrest Bible College, Caronport, Saskatchewan, Canada

"Whenever I preach a sermon in the first person, the most common response is 'When are you going to do that again?' First-person narrative grabs the attention of the entire audience. Children's workers ask to let the small children stay for the sermon because it holds the interest of everyone. The only complaint that I have ever had when I do this form of message is that I don't do it often enough."

—Mike Jaskilka, Berean Baptist, Eugene, Oregon

"The beauty of first-person narrative is the element of surprise—by the time the congregation dials in to what's going on—you've got them—undivided."

—Doug Green, North Hills Church, Brea, California

"If I had to make my living from acting, I would have starved a long time ago. It's for that very reason that the course requirement insisting that I preach a first-person narrative left my nerves frayed and my stomach churning. I elected to embody Pilate in the story of Good Friday. What overwhelmed me more than anything else was the impact that the sermon had on the hearts of my people. For a number of weeks, people stopped me to tell me that the narrative let them see and feel the drama of Jesus' trial like nothing else before. They saw Jesus with their own eyes and they loved him more for his sacrifice. So, if a left-brained preacher like me can do it—you ought to do it! Do it for the sake of your congregation. Do it for the sake of Christ."

—Lech Bekesza, Cobble Hill Baptist Church,
Cobble Hill, British Columbia, Canada

"I was totally amazed at the response of our church family the first time I delivered a first-person sermon. People could not wait for me to do another one."

—Kent Hinkel, First Baptist Church, Minot, North Dakota

"No other method of sermon presentation has caught and kept the attention of my congregation like first-person narrative. It is dramatic in its presentation, biblical in its premise, pragmatic in its purpose, and motivational in its approach. First-person narrative quickens the congregation to the truthfulness of Scripture, making the text come to life in the believer's heart."

—Chaplain (Lieutenant Colonel) Jay Hartranft,
173d Airborne Brigade, U.S. Army

"I was surprised by the overwhelming positive response to my first-person narrative on Gideon from Judges 5–6. People said things like: 'I saw Gideon,' 'I will never forget this story,' 'That was great,' and 'When are you going to do this again?'"

—Bob Lundgren, Wawasee Community Bible Church,
Milford, Indiana

"Because I live in a small fishing port on Canada's east coast, when I was wondering how to go about preaching a first-person narrative, Jonah came quite naturally. A local costume shop outfitted me as Jonah, and I told his/my story as if I had come up through time and was 'cast ashore' so to speak. The congregation loved it and talked about it for weeks."

—John Carroll, Dipper Harbour United Baptist Church,
Dipper Harbour, New Brunswick, Canada

"Using the first-person sermon has had a dramatic impact on my preaching ministry. I have found that it both disarms my listeners and arrests their attention like no other kind of message. An example would be the first one I did as Cain. I stood before the people and asked them if they had ever done anything terrible in their lives, something that others would be absolutely shocked to discover. I then said, 'As difficult as it is to confess, I feel that I must tell you about something horrible I have done.' At this point I saw some tissues dabbing eyes, as people anticipated a moral failure. Deacons squirmed in their seat, probably wondering why I hadn't told them first. I then said, 'You see . . . I've killed my brother.' There was a collective sigh of relief because the congregation knew I didn't have a brother. But I did have their attention!"

—Kevin Brennan, Evangel Church, Scotch Plains, New Jersey

"I have come to realize more fully that creativity and imagination are not incongruous to effective expository preaching but are actually essential to it. A preacher refusing to make use of first-person narrative sermons is like a football team failing to include the forward pass among their offensive weapons. By unnecessarily limiting the ways in which you can carry God's truth to its goal, the end zone of people's hearts and minds is reached less often."

—Michael Butzberger, Lighthouse Baptist Church, North Palm Beach, Florida

"The sermon my congregation remembers best is a first-person sermon in which I took the part of Simeon from Luke 2. That was over four years ago. I recently preached a first-person sermon based on Mark 10:46–52, and, interpret this as you will, the congregation applauded when it was over."

—Michael Malanga, Emmanuel Congregational Church, Ridgetown, Ontario, Canada

"I recently preached through the Book of Acts as Peter, as the Philippian jailer, and as Paul before Festus and Agrippa. First-person narrative preaching brought me new insights into God's truth and helped me say things about Scripture in a fresh and penetrating way. I've overcome any fear of first-person narratives and wish I had learned to preach them fifteen years earlier in my ministry!"

—The Rev. John M. Heidengren, Prince of Peace Episcopal Church, Aliquippa, Pennsylvania

2

Preaching As Listeners Like It

The reporter stood in the crowd and stuck his microphone in the face of a man standing nearby. "Many people say," the reporter began, "that the problem with our country today is that its citizens are ignorant and apathetic. Tell me, sir," the journalist queried, "what do you think?"

The man responded, "I don't know and I don't care."

Ask the average man or woman on the street to define first-person preaching or expository preaching, and you will most likely get a similar response. Ask the typical person in the pew and you may get a blank stare. They don't know and they don't care. Even among preachers who have some understanding of expository preaching and who may be aware of first-person preaching, few believe the terms "first person" and "expository" can both describe the same sermon.

First-person expository preaching suffers on three counts. Most churchgoers are not accustomed to any regular biblical exposition from the pulpit, relatively few have heard a first-person sermon, and fewer still have listened to a first-person expository sermon.

Yet people who have heard a good first-person expository sermon often never forget it. First-person exposition combines the power of drama with the authority of the Word of God. Those who are acquainted with this form of preaching know its effectiveness. At the outset then, it is important to understand what a first-person expository sermon is and to appreciate what makes it effective.

What Is an Expository First-Person Sermon?

To define an expository first-person sermon, we need to explore each of its parts.

Expository. Common to most of the definitions is that the message of the sermon is derived from a text of Scripture. The definition of exposition that we will be using is from Harold Freeman: An expository sermon is one which "confronts the hearers with an accurate interpretation of the biblical revelation and its present meaning for their lives."[1]

First-person. A first-person sermon (sometimes referred to as a dramatic monologue) is a sermon preached from the viewpoint of an eyewitness to a biblical event. First-person sermons recount a story from the perspective of one of the characters in the story.

The expository first-person sermon form is based on an accurate interpretation of Scripture and applies its meaning to the hearers. It does this through the retelling of the scriptural account from the vantage point of a character who was part of the story.

Why Preach a First-Person Expository Sermon?

Defining our terms helps to make the unfamiliar a bit more familiar. But the question remains, why go through the trouble of learning a new sermon form?

First-person expository sermons communicate their message through *the power of story* and *the power of drama* working together. That is why a good first-person biblical sermon is likely to be among the most effective you will ever preach and among the most memorable your listeners will ever hear.

The Power of Story

People remember good stories. A first-person sermon tells a story from an insider's perspective. Experienced preachers know that often what people remember most from their sermons are the illustrations. Listeners struggle to remember the sermon's points, but they are likely to remember the preacher's stories.[2]

We live in a story culture. The men and women who sit in church on Sunday live their lives in a society dominated by story. The average person spends about twenty-seven hours each week watching television, and television is a medium of story. Each thirty-minute sitcom is a story. Every newscast is composed of news "stories." Even the sporting events portrayed on television are embellished with stories. Sportscasters come on the air thirty minutes before the game to tell the story surrounding the game. Throughout the game they fill in the minutes telling stories about the athletes. And when people take a break from television, occasionally they watch stories conveyed through motion pictures.

Stories enable listeners to experience the truth of God in their lives. The film industry uses the term "emotional truth" to refer to the broad message of a film, which, combined with artistic production, makes the audience connect with its theme. Good stories relate truth to our experiences and cause it to touch both our minds and our hearts. Stories connect truth to life.

Stories paint mental pictures that influence the way people think. People are influenced, not by abstract concepts, but by pictures painted by stories that hang in the galleries of their minds. Fred Craddock explains:

> Images are replaced not by concepts but by other images, and that quite slowly. Long after a man's head has consented to the preacher's idea, the old images may still hang in the heart. But not until that image is replaced is he really a changed man; until then he is a torn man, doing battle with himself and possibly making casualties of those nearby in the process. This change takes time, because the longest trip a person takes is that from head to heart.[3]

Stories reflect the way people experience life. Stories are inductive. They move from the specific to the general, from many specific instances to a broad moral or lesson. Because stories are inductive, they reflect life. Life is lived inductively. We seldom think about mortality in the abstract. We usually think about it when a young friend dies suddenly or when we read an obituary in the paper and the person who died was seven years younger than we are. We experience life a second at a time. Out of all the experiences of our lives, we learn the broad lessons life teaches.

The Power of Drama

Because the preacher uses the perspective of an insider in delivering a first-person message, the sermon has about it a strong dramatic element. Like any drama, it involves people in conflict and resolution. Because of this dramatic element, first-person sermons can be educational, inspirational, and at the same time engaging.

A Form for All Seasons

Ministers can preach first-person expository sermons throughout the year and employ elements of first-person preaching in more traditional sermons. While they are particularly effective at Christmas or Easter, they can be used at other times in the church year.

Ministers can use them to communicate the message of a narrative passage as well as to bring the New Testament epistles to life.[4] Behind the letters in the New Testament, there is always someone writing and someone reading. How would Peter or Paul or John have talked about their epistles? How would a member of a congregation in Galatia have reacted to the angry, passionate letter he or she received from Paul? Answering these questions is the stuff of first-person preaching.

First-person expository sermons can speak to people not only in the seasons of the church year but also in the seasons of their lives. They appeal to children and teenagers who love to hear a story. They speak to men and women in their noontime years who wonder how God's truth intersects with their careers and families. First-person sermons speak to people in their later years because they bring old truth home in a fresh way.

Summary

While you may not be familiar with first-person expository sermons, you will discover they are well suited to communicate God's truth effectively to twenty-first-century listeners. This sermon form offers a powerful tool for the preacher who wants to communicate the biblical message in a relevant and dramatic way to a culture shaped by story.

3

Study! Study! Study!

J. H. Jowett, in his 1912 Yale lectures on preaching, quoted the adage of a venerable English judge: "Cases are won in chambers." For an attorney, the success of his case is determined largely by the diligence of his preparation. The same applies to the preacher. Jowett explained, "If the study is a lounge, the pulpit will be an impertinence."[1] Good expository preaching requires diligent preparation. This is especially true when preparing a first-person expository sermon.

Selecting a Biblical Text

The debate still rages over which came first, the chicken or the egg. The reality is that you can't have one without the other. Similarly, first-person exposition requires both a character and a biblical text. Sometimes as you study a particular text, a vantage point suggested by the text will be intriguing. For example, when contemplating a sermon on the parable of the prodigal son, you may recognize that the story could be told from the perspective of one of several different people: the boy who ran off to a far country, the father who waited patiently at home, the older brother who took care of the farm, or even a nosy next-door neighbor. In the study process, the text may guide you to a character.

Most often first-person sermons will be born from your interest in a particular biblical figure. The Bible is filled with flawed heroes and cunning villains. The personalities of the Bible have inspired innumerable sermons. The church calendar may bring certain characters to mind. The Christmas season, for example, might suggest a sermon from the perspective of Mary, Joseph, Herod, the wise men, or one of the other characters involved in the story of Christ's coming to earth. Easter might prompt a visit from Peter, Thomas, Mary Magdalene, an angel, or one of the other witnesses to the resurrection.[2] In these cases, having identified a character, you then go in search of a text.

Whether a biblical passage suggests a character or the choice of a character leads to a text, in an expository sermon the biblical text must shape the sermon. A valid criticism of many first-person sermons is that they don't take the text seriously. It is easy for a first-person preacher to, in Elizabeth Achtemeier's words, "psychologize the text," adding details which alter and lead to a misinterpretation of the Scripture.[3] Accurately communicating the message of the biblical writer should be your utmost concern as a first-person expositor.

If you have a character in mind, you are likely well on your way to choosing a preaching text. If you don't have a character in mind, two other factors are critical to the selection of any preaching passage. When choosing a text from which to preach, it is wise to keep in mind both the needs of your audience and any needs relevant to the occasion on which you will be speaking. While all Scripture is profitable, not all passages possess equal profit for a particular congregation at a particular time.

Excellent preaching texts for first-person sermons abound throughout the Bible. Biblical narratives are often ideally suited for first-person sermons. The testimonies of men like Caleb (Josh. 14:6–15), Nebuchadnezzar (Dan. 4), and Paul (Acts 22:3–21; 24:10b–21; 26:2–23; 28:17b–20; Gal. 1–2) are conveyed by the biblical writers in first-person form, so it is a relatively easy task to craft a first-person sermon from such passages.[4] Most biblical narratives are recorded in the third person, but ministers can still communicate these stories forcefully to a modern audience in the form of a first-person sermon. For example, the story of Ruth is written from a third-person perspective by a narrator who was not part of the events about which he writes. But the story could be retold from the vantage point of a character who did have a part in the events—characters such as Ruth herself, fellow gleaners in the field, Naomi, Boaz, or Boaz's harvesters.[5]

Biblical narrative is not the only source for first-person sermons. Psalm 73, while poetry, is the testimony of a worship leader who almost lost his faith. It can make a memorable first-person sermon. The pithy truth of a proverb can become palpable to a contemporary audience when illustrated in a story told from a first-person perspective.[6] John's vision on the Island of Patmos found in the Book of Revelation is clearly prophetic literature, and yet it is also his personal experience. Often a first-person sermon can remove some of the mystery that shrouds prophetic literature. With careful exegesis poetry, prophecy, wisdom literature, parables, and epistles may all be preached effectively from a first-person perspective.

As you endeavor to select a text, the passage you choose must contain a complete unit of thought. In the New Testament letters, a unit of thought is a paragraph or more. In poetry it is a stanza. In narrative, a complete unit of thought is either an entire story or an episode within the story. To interpret a story properly, you must determine where it begins and where it ends. Accurate exegesis demands that you select an entire story, a whole paragraph, or a complete unit of thought, not just a fragment of a text.[7]

Having chosen a text, what's the next step?

Exegesis

Before you can develop your sermon, you need to understand what the passage you have selected actually teaches. Exegesis is the process by which this is done. Exegesis is an art as well as a science, so the process involved in the study of a passage will not always follow an exact pattern. What's more, the kind of exegesis involved in discovering the main idea of a passage will differ depending on the genre of the biblical literature. The method for understanding and interpreting poetry is different from that used for letters, which is different again from that used for prophecy, and so on.[8]

Nevertheless, in preparing a first-person expository sermon, the following three exegetical tasks are important to the exegesis of any biblical genre.

1. Determine the Exegetical Idea

The first task in exegesis is to determine the main idea of the text. Frequently, the main thrust of the text does not emerge until after you have overturned all the exegetical stones. Sometimes the idea emerges in the middle of your exegetical spadework. Wherever it comes in the process, determining the main idea of the text is the primary objective of exegesis. At the same time, unearthing the main idea of the passage is often the most demanding step you take in the preparation of an expository sermon. But you must mine the gold before you can mint it into spendable currency. Without a clear understanding of the central idea of a biblical text, you have nothing to say.

To find the main idea, it is helpful to know what you're looking for. Every idea can be broken down into a subject and complement. The subject can be phrased in the form of a question and presents a problem to be solved by the complement. The complement *completes* the subject.

For example, the Book of Ruth tells the story of ordinary people who, during the period of the judges, a time of moral chaos, were faithful to others and to God. By virtue of the faithfulness of Boaz and Ruth, God met the dire needs of Ruth and Naomi and ultimately brought about the birth of Israel's greatest king. The idea of that story is that God makes a difference to those who are faithful to God and to his people. It could be broken down into a subject and complement like this:

Subject: How does God make a difference through ordinary people?

Complement: God works through their faithfulness to himself and to others.

The story of the selection of David as king and the account of his battle with Goliath in 1 Samuel 16–17 tells us something important about leaders. Spiritual leadership is not a matter of age or physical stature. God chose Israel's second king by a different standard. The exegetical idea is that the man called to be king demonstrated courage that came from a vital faith in God. It could also be stated as a subject and complement:

Subject: What did God look for in the man he chose to lead his people?
Complement: David demonstrated courage that grew out of a vital faith in God.

In response to two brothers who were arguing over money, Jesus told a story about a man who put his fortune in real estate. The parable of the rich fool in Luke 12 is a tale of a man who was financially set but spiritually destitute. The idea of the parable of the rich fool is that those who leave God out of their lives will ultimately have nothing. Here is a subject-complement breakdown:

Subject: What happened to the man who had no time for God in his life?
Complement: The investment of his life came to nothing.

Precisely stating the main idea of your text in the form of a subject and a complement is hard work, but this idea is the gold for which you are digging in the exegetical process. If you have stated it accurately, your main idea should fit all the details of the biblical passage. This exegetical idea is the key that unlocks the meaning of the text.[9]

2. Research the Character or Characters

In the process of exegesis, your second task is to research the characters in the text. A study of both the characters in the text and the geographical, historical, and cultural situation of the text are essential for a first-person expository sermon. This is true even if the passage you are preaching is not narrative and even if you have already determined its main idea. Details about the biblical characters and their setting add color and believability to your sermon. On the other hand, if your listeners recognize inaccuracies in your description of the character or the setting, they have reason to wonder about the trustworthiness of the rest of your message. Worse yet, if they don't recognize such inaccuracies, they are likely to believe and propagate your errors.

As a Bible expositor, it is imperative that you allow the text to speak for itself before crafting your sermon. This involves hearing from all the witnesses. Especially when searching for the main idea in narrative literature, a study of a story's different characters often provides an important piece for solving the story's puzzle.

It may seem like keen insight into the obvious, but when researching a character, begin with the Bible. When doing this, you will benefit from good study tools. A concordance, Bible handbook, Bible encyclopedia, Bible dictionary, and biographical studies may each come in handy.

It is essential to have a good concordance. Look up the different biblical references on your character and make note of the qualities and attributes that emerge. It is often worthwhile to note the various references to your character by the same biblical writer. For example, John paints a consistent picture of the disciple known to us as "doubting Thomas."

Most people know Thomas only by his skeptical statement in John 20:25: "Unless I see the nail marks in his hands and put my finger where the nails were, and put my hand into his side, I will not believe it." But John uses this incident not to condemn Thomas but rather to demonstrate to his readers the believability of Jesus as the Christ. Throughout John's Gospel, Thomas tells it like it is. According to John's account, Thomas was the disciple who spoke up when Jesus determined to go to Bethany, about two miles from Jerusalem, because of the death of his friend Lazarus. Not long before, on Jesus' last visit to Jerusalem with his disciples, the Jews tried to stone Jesus. Knowing the danger, Thomas responds to Jesus' seemingly foolhardy plan: "Let us also go, that we may die with him" (John 11:16). Thomas was faithful but forthright. The consistency of Thomas's candor is evident once again in John 14 when he was the only disciple who dared to ask Jesus what he was talking about when Jesus spoke of returning to his Father's house: "Thomas said to him, 'Lord, we don't know where you are going, so how can we know the way?'" (v. 5). Thomas was not especially prone to doubt. He was a man who spoke his mind, and frankly he couldn't believe that Jesus had risen from the dead just because his friends thought so. As with Thomas, by searching other pertinent Scriptures with the aid of a concordance, you will be able to gain a fuller understanding of your character.

Also consult articles in Bible handbooks, encyclopedias, and dictionaries. In researching your character, the following details are worth exploring:

- the character's background
- where he or she grew up
- the kind of home he or she grew up in
- his or her socioeconomic background
- the function of the character in the drama
- any distinguishing physical characteristics or traits

As you do your research, it is helpful to "get inside the head" of your character. How does your character think? What drives him or her? The following characteristics are also worth investigating:

- *Basic attitudes*. What are the character's likes and dislikes when it comes to life or other characters in the story?
- *Social style*. Is he or she combative or friendly, gregarious or antisocial?
- *Emotional makeup*. Is he or she quick tempered or self-controlled? Caring or spiteful? Steady or imbalanced?
- *Moral and ethical development*. Where is the character at this stage of his or her spiritual pilgrimage?
- *Inner motivations*. What drives this character?
- *Distinguishing qualities*. Is the character old or young, rich or poor, intelligent or foolish, meticulous or unkempt? Are there any other unique traits? How is this character like you or different from you?

Biographical studies will also help you familiarize yourself with your character.[10] You may find historical fiction by responsible writers helpful, provided you are able to distinguish fact from fiction as you read it.[11]

To put all this information about your character together, think of writing a paragraph or two describing your character. If you were studying the prophet Elijah, you might sum up your findings like this:

> The prophet Elijah is one of the most widely recognized Old Testament characters, yet it's surprising how much we don't know about him. First Kings 17:1 says he was a Tishbite who was one of the inhabitants of Gilead. We know he was a Tishbite, but we're not quite sure where in Gilead Tishbe was. His name stands out, for Elijah means "The LORD is God" (or "Yahweh is God"), but we don't know how he got that name. We don't know who his parents were, nor do we know anything about his background. Much about the prophet is shrouded in mystery. Elijah simply bursts onto the scene in 1 Kings 17.
>
> What we do know about Elijah is that he stands out as one of the most passionate characters of the Bible. Elijah tended to run either hot or cold. He stood up and boldly confronted the prophets of Baal on Mount Carmel, but then when Queen Jezebel threatened to kill him, Elijah fled into the wilderness and pled with God to take his life. His name sums up his ministry, for the prophet confronted the wayward nation and its king with the fact that Jehovah was God. Finally, after performing some of the most amazing miracles in the Old Testament, including raising a young man from the dead, Elijah literally disappeared into heaven in a fiery chariot.

Summarizing your character in this way will record and help clarify what you have learned.

3. Research the Setting

Your third exegetical task is researching the setting described or suggested by the text. Every first-person sermon has a historical and geographical "zip code." It concerns a particular place and specific time. The *cultural, historical,* and *geographical* details you uncover regarding the setting of your passage will make for more accurate exegesis and more descriptive preaching. A Bible atlas and Bible commentary may prove useful in this area.

Geography is important in understanding the setting of a passage. Where did a recorded event take place? Was it in the mountains? Was it beside a lake or in the desert? If the characters move from one place to another, how far did they have to travel? Can you locate their destination on a map? A Bible atlas will show the way.

Until the early nineteenth century and the invention of the steam engine, no one could travel more than eight miles per hour. Two centuries ago in the United States, if a family moved from Massachusetts to Pennsylvania, their friends in Massachusetts never expected to see them again. Likewise, in the ancient world seemingly small distances made a big difference. A sprinkling of geographical information can add zest to any sermon. It is a particularly important ingredient in first-person exposition.

It is equally important to be acquainted with the *historical* and *cultural* setting depicted by a passage. What was life like for Abraham, David, or Samson? What were the social, political, and intellectual constraints of the time? Take a mental snapshot of the cultural and historical situation described by the text. Two basic questions may guide you in this study: How did life then resemble life today? And how did it differ?

A good Bible commentary will often provide you with insight into some of the historical and cultural issues that impact the understanding of a portion of Scripture. A Bible handbook, dictionary, or encyclopedia may also provide information to help you in this task.

As you endeavor to understand the geographical, historical, and cultural context of your passage, consider the following features of setting:

Weather and Climate

If you want your listeners to enter fully into the story with you, you have to step into it yourself. As you observe the scene, what was the weather like? Was it hot or cold, rainy or dry? While familiarity with the ancient weather patterns will not always be necessary to understand a passage, in some biblical stories knowledge of weather and climate is essential.

Critics impressed by the movie *The Perfect Storm* claimed that the central figure of the film was not Billy Tyne, captain of the fishing boat, but the menacing storm itself. By use of amazing special effects, the movie's producers cast the storm as the central character. So it is in Luke's action-packed account of Paul's voyage to Rome in Acts 27–28. Due to the danger of severe weather, sailing the Mediterranean in the fall was dangerous and ill advised for ancient mariners. Traveling by ship in the winter was practically suicidal. Luke alerts his readers to the danger that lay ahead when he explains that the ship carrying himself, Paul, and 274 others did not set sail from Crete until after Yom Kippur. Due to a severe, unexpected fall storm, the only destination for this ship would be the bottom of the Mediterranean.

Storms of the type described by Luke are familiar to folks who live in New England. Unlike normal air currents, these gale-force winds are driven from the Northeast, giving them their name, "northeasters." New Englanders refer to them as "nor'easters." Meteorologists, aware of their destructive power, have another name for them. They call them "bombs."

Luke records that the ship gave way to the wind. This made for a terrifying ride. As they plunged off the top of a great wind-driven wave, they felt the water flow out from under them. Like a roller coaster gone wild, the boat just dropped. If the ship could have taken the seas head on, at least they could have seen what was coming at them while the gale blew past. Instead, they were drenched, beaten, and battered, driven by the storm for fourteen days.

Knowing something about storms at sea helps you and your listeners see the dark and violent waves and feel the sting of the rain and the force of the gale. A little information about weather and climate can paint a sensational picture.

Habits and Customs

Study of some biblical texts will necessitate that you explore the worship practices of the people in the ancient world. How did they worship? Where did they worship? In Jesus' parable of the tax collector and the Pharisee in Luke 18, Luke tells us that both the Pharisee and the tax collector went up to the temple to pray. The Pharisee stood up to pray, but the tax collector stood at a distance. Jesus' audience, familiar with the layout of the temple, could picture the scene. Modern audiences need help.

The Jewish temple was an impressive structure, designed to remind people of the holy nature of God. At the center of the temple was the Most Holy Place, where the ark containing the stone tablets of Moses was kept. The ark symbolized the very presence of God. Gentiles could not get close to it and were kept at a distance. Jewish women could proceed past the court of the Gentiles, but could go no closer. Jewish men could proceed past the court of the women, but could not enter the Holy Place. Only priests who had been ceremonially cleansed could enter the Holy Place to represent the people before God. And only one man, the high priest, could enter the Most Holy Place, once each year. The temple was designed to keep sinful people at a distance from their holy God.

The Pharisee in Jesus' story, proud of his great moral achievements, strode pompously into the temple, past the court of the Gentiles, through the court of the women and stood proudly in the court of the men, not far from the Holy Place. In contrast, both the posture and the position of the tax collector reveal a man who felt profoundly unworthy to come before God. His downcast eyes evidenced his sense of guilt. He beat on his breast like a woman in grief. While the Pharisee stood confidently near the Holy Place in the temple, the tax collector stood off at a distance on the fringes of the court of the men, overwhelmed by his sinfulness. He was repentant and broken. His distance from the place of God's presence suggests the tax collector's sense of unworthiness. Both men stood before God, but only the tax collector saw himself in relation to God's holiness. Understanding the temple layout can help your listeners understand what Jesus said.

A different sermon may require you to answer a different set of questions: What type of food did they eat? How was it prepared? What did they wear? How did they farm? What did they grow and how was it planted and harvested? The writer of Ruth shrouds the details of the incident at the threshing floor in secrecy. But you can help illuminate what happened in that

Judean night if you have a clear mental picture of the threshing process and what an ancient threshing floor looked like.

To understand the life and customs of the ancient world, you may need to know now what they knew then. How did they understand their world? Did they have any scientific understanding? What was medical care like? What were the technological advances of the day?

In the days of the judges, the Amalekites were a military power because they had a strategic weapon, the camel. Because their camels could travel long distances with relative speed and minimal water, the Amalekites had long-range attack capability. In David's day, the Philistines had military superiority. J. Kent Edwards explains in a narrative sermon preached from the perspective of Eliab, David's older brother:

> The Philistines were not nice people. They had an unfair military advantage. They knew how to smelt iron. That allowed them to make weapons, swords and javelins that allowed them to have superiority on the battlefield. Well, they'd used their smelting of iron for our benefit, but only in terms of agricultural implements. They wanted us to be able to grow more food, so they could come steal it. But on the battlefield, they had us beat, every time. And even though they belonged on the seacoast, they kept coming in farther and farther, making encroaches into our land. They knew that we were a bunch of farmers, that we couldn't stop them.[12]

The ancient story connects with our life's story when we understand what they understood.

Archaeology

What pertinent information is available from archaeological discoveries? Dusty archaeological data can breathe life into a first-person sermon. For example, while King Herod is always cast as the villain in Christmas pageants, historians and archaeologists remember him for his building projects. If you were to schedule an interview with Herod, it wouldn't be surprising if he wanted to talk about some of these impressive achievements. You might ask King Herod to tell you about the killing of the infants recorded in Matthew. And he might reply:

> You want to bring that up, do you? You want to ignore all the things I did that made me great. You want to ignore that I was a great builder. During the forty-one years of my reign, I built theaters, amphitheaters, hippodromes. I introduced athletic games in honor of Caesar. I constructed cities and rebuilt fortresses. They were important, lasting public works projects. I built palaces throughout the country. I built Jewish temples in Gentile territory.
>
> Even today you can see the magnificent ruins of what I built in Israel. I started the rebuilding of the Jewish temple in Jerusalem. It took eighty-eight years to complete. I used massive stones to build it. The dome of the temple was covered with gold. Pilgrims climbing up to the temple had to shield their eyes. The dome was like the sun. One rabbi said of that temple, "If you have not seen the temple in Jerusalem, then you have never seen a beautiful building." They refer to that structure as Herod's Temple. That's what made me great. But you don't think about that at all. That tax collector, Matthew, never mentions it. All you want to talk about are those astrologers and that baby.[13]

The archaeologist's spade brings splashes of color to a first-person sermon.

Social Structure

What kinds of social, racial, and sexual barriers existed when your story took place? Essential to understanding the New Testament is the recognition of the intense animosity between Jews and Samaritans. You cannot grasp the significance of Jesus' parable of the good Samaritan without this awareness.

More than seven hundred years before Christ's birth, the Assyrian war machine marched into Israel and deported the Israelites to Assyria. As was their custom, the Assyrians forced the Israelites to intermarry with people from the surrounding pagan nations and repopulated the part of Israel known as Samaria with men and women from other nations and with these intermarried or "half-breed" Jews. The Jews of Judea looked upon Samaritans as a mongrel race. These people of diluted race developed a religion that was an amalgam of Judaism and paganism.

Given this history, it is not surprising that the Jews and the Samaritans hated each other. Gary Inrig conveys the depth of their animosity:

> We call this the story of "the good Samaritan," but to first-century Jews there was no such thing. This was as unthinkable as the good PLO member to the Zionist, the good IRA member to a North Irish Ulsterman, the good African National Congress follower to the Afrikaaner. The animosity between Jew and Samaritan was intense. The Jews believed that the Samaritans had defiled the temple, distorted the Torah, and degraded divine worship. Although he spoke two centuries later, Rabbi Shimon ben Jochai's words convey the attitude of first-century Jews toward their Samaritan neighbors. "They have no law, not even the remnants of a command, and are thus suspect and degenerate." For their part, the Samaritans returned the hostility in full measure.[14]

To first-century Jews, casting a Samaritan as the hero in any story was outrageous. Without an awareness of the social, racial, and sexual tensions that existed in the ancient world, modern audiences are unlikely to feel the intended impact of the biblical story.

City and Rural Life

Help your listeners experience what life was like in the country villages and urban centers of the biblical world. For example, when Onesimus, the escaped slave of Philemon, fled to Rome, what would he have seen as he entered that great city? Onesimus must have been impressed by the huge, diverse, cosmopolitan population of the city. Men and women from every nation filled the streets, dressed in exotic garb, speaking a Babel of languages. Sprinkled around the city he saw temples of native and imported gods, pyramids and obelisks from Egypt, statues and paintings from Greece, and warehouses holding grain and goods from Africa, Spain, and Gaul.

No doubt, Onesimus stopped to take in the immense Colosseum, scene of great athletic contests and gladiatorial games. He walked wide-eyed through the forum. He may have noted the basilica where Roman lawyers argued their cases and Italian businessmen negotiated their deals. He may have paused to admire the Senate House, home of the Roman Senate, or the great temple of Jupiter situated atop the Capitoline Hill. In every corner of the city, Onesimus would have been impressed by the many monuments proclaiming the power, traditions, and breadth of the Roman Empire.[15] A few well-chosen details can bring your listeners with you on the trip through the city streets and country fields of the ancient world.

Government

People in the West can tend to assume that everyone shares their experience of living in a free and open society. But around the world and throughout history, governments and political systems have been as different as communism and democracy. Because of that, as you preach stories from the ancient world, you are likely to benefit from knowing about the rulers and political structures of that day. What was the government like? Who was in charge? How did it differ from our experience?

In his letter to the Romans, Paul writes, "Everyone must submit himself to governing authorities, for there is no authority except that which God has established" (Rom. 13:1). It is easy for us to wonder whether that applies to us today. But Paul wrote those words as a Roman citizen, under Roman rule.

In the Roman world, the emperor was more than a ruler. He was worshiped as a god. And the emperor in power when Paul wrote to the Romans was the infamous Nero. Although Nero began well under Seneca's guidance, he became increasingly despotic after he murdered his mother, Agripinna. He used the fire that destroyed much of Rome as a pretext to persecute Christians. Nero would tie Christians to posts, cover their bodies with pitch and burn them as human torches to light his garden parties. Ultimately, it was under Nero that Paul was beheaded.

Paul's instruction to the Romans, of course, is not an endorsement of the atrocities committed by the Roman emperor. Nero and Stalin, Hitler and Osama bin Laden will all be judged one day by the King of kings. Nevertheless, Paul affirms the authority of the Roman government, even under Nero, as an instrument of God to uphold justice and peace in society. If Paul's instruction applied to the ruling power in his day, it surely applies in ours. Christians are to submit to the authorities who provide protection and maintain order in our community and our country. If the great apostle were to step out of the pages of Scripture and speak to Americans or Canadians or English citizens today, would he give us different instructions? Probably not. Awareness of the political world of his day clarifies and reinforces what he would say to us.

Flora and Fauna

Study of the plant and animal life in the ancient world may sound like the reflections of someone with too much time on his hands, but significant insight can sprout from a little research. When Jesus preached about fig trees and sowing seed, the people of his day listened attentively. Modern audiences will listen with greater interest when you provide them with relevant insights into the plants and animals of the ancient world.

On numerous occasions the fig tree is mentioned in the Bible. Few Americans have fig trees growing in their yards, but figs are native to the Mediterranean area and formed an important part of the diet of ancient civilizations in the Near East. They are mentioned as one of the seven fruits of the Promised Land. So while the fig tree may seem somewhat foreign to us, it was every bit as familiar to the people of the Old and New Testaments as the apple tree is to people in the northern United States:

> Figs may be eaten fresh or dried, but the first ripe fig was reckoned a very tasty morsel. . . . In the dried state, figs were an important food all year round and valuable in wartime, especially during sieges. Supplies were stored in fortified strongholds such as Masada, where remnants have been found during excavations. The best figs were dried individually. The second best were strung together and dried, while ordinary figs were pressed together in lumps. These caked figs were commonplace and ready at hand; hence Abigail could send David two hundred cakes of figs together with other offerings.[16]

If you wanted to tell the story of David and Abigail or one of the other biblical accounts in which figs are mentioned, some of this information might prove helpful. You will better communicate the teaching of much of the Scriptures to people today if you and they are better acquainted with the common plant and animal life of the Bible.

Time

As you picture the setting of the biblical story for your listeners, what time of day is it? Was the sun high overhead or was it disappearing on the horizon? What time of year was it? As in Paul's voyage to Rome, sometimes the season of the year is essential to the story. Whether or not time is a factor in the biblical account, accurately detailing the time and the season adds greater depth to your story.

Money

"A penny saved is a penny earned." That famous saying of Benjamin Franklin has been proven false. Due to inflation, the penny you saved twenty years ago has lost almost all of its buying power today. Back in the 1960s a dime could buy a Coke from a vending machine or make a local call from a pay phone. Today, that same phone call will cost at least thirty-five cents, and you'll need ten dimes to buy a soft drink from most vending machines.

When telling biblical stories, it is imperative to your listeners' understanding that you convert denarii to dollars, but that may not be enough. The changing value of money makes it critical that you look for equivalent values in today's currency. In the story of the good Samaritan in Luke 10, the Samaritan gave the innkeeper money to care for the Jewish mugging victim. How much cash did he leave with the innkeeper?

The New International Version of the Bible tells us, "He took out two silver coins and gave them to the innkeeper" (Luke 10:35). The New American Standard Bible says, "He took out two denarii and gave them to the innkeeper." With either translation, we have no idea how much he shelled out in today's currency. But the margin of the NASB tells us that the denarius was equivalent to a day's wage. If the average worker's hourly wage today in the United States is over $10, the Samaritan would have spent at least $160 on this stranger. People can appreciate the generosity of the Samaritan when it is translated into terms they can grasp.

Weights and Measures

As with money, ancient Near-Eastern systems of measurement must be translated to units your audience can understand.

Yet even when you use the correct English or metric system equivalent, the measure may still be unclear to your listeners. In the story of Ruth, according to both the NIV and the NASB, when Ruth returned to Naomi from the threshing floor, Boaz gave Ruth "six measures" of barley (Ruth 3:15). How much is that?

Steve Mathewson, in his sermon from Ruth, translates this unfamiliar amount into an English equivalent: "more than half a bushel." Yet even this measurement is unclear to people accustomed to buying their products by the pound or by the box. So Mathewson restates this in terms all his listeners can understand: "When she finished the day, she had over a half a bushel—a phenomenal amount for one day's work! And food enough for several days!"[17] Bushels, pecks, or pounds, weights and measures communicated in terms your audience understands provide the sort of specific detail of which good stories are made.

From weather and climate to weights and measures, researching the geographical, historical, and cultural situation is a lot of ground to cover. You will not necessarily explore each of these topics for every first-person sermon, but knowledge of the story's setting will help you resurrect the past for your listeners.

Summary

Kent Edwards warns, "Creative presentation of the text is no excuse for sloppy interpretation of the text."[18] A good expository first-person sermon is built upon solid exegesis. Researching the historical situation and characters in the text will help unlock the main idea of the text. At the same time, this material can also enrich the sermon and strengthen its impact on those who hear it.

4

O Say Can You See?

Somewhere in the exegetical process, you must decide which person to portray. Frequently this will be one of the major characters of the Bible. Listeners are likely to take note when King David, Queen Esther, or the Apostle Paul fills the pulpit.

But sometimes a minor biblical character may tell the story. In a society of trivia buffs, many listeners would be intrigued to hear an account from a bit player such as Eliab,[1] Dorcas, or Tychicus. These characters do not necessarily relate their personal stories. Instead they provide a viewpoint on the biblical passage. The thrust of the text determines the essence of the story. The best choice of character therefore is the one who most effectively conveys the substance of the text.

If you choose not to use major or minor biblical characters to tell the story, an imaginary character may work well. The historical and cultural research you have done in exegesis will prove helpful in creating a believable character. This imaginary figure might be a real person about whom the biblical text says little or nothing. For example, you might introduce the Book of Philippians from the perspective of a first-century Roman guard. Paul was under house arrest in Rome, chained to different members of the Praetorian Guard as he wrote the letter. The imaginary character might also be someone who never really existed, but whose imaginary existence is consistent with the details of the passage and the realities of the historical setting. For example, in the sermon "Simon Said" from Luke 12 (Appendix 5), Alice Mathews tells Jesus' story of the rich fool from the perspective of the wealthy man's widow.

Once you have selected your character, you must answer two critical questions of that character: Who is he and why is he here? The answers to these two questions will determine the character's personality and his or her stance in relation to the audience. This leads to the next step in preparing a first-person expository sermon.

Determine the Character's Personality and Stance

Who Am I?

The work you have already done in the exegetical process will have gone a long way in answering the first critical question, "Who am I?" When you have done the exegetical research on the character, you will benefit from writing a summary paragraph of all the data compiled on the character, as mentioned in the last chapter. This paragraph will read something like an article in an encyclopedia. There is both a short-term and long-term benefit to this exercise. The short-term benefit is that writing this paragraph will begin to crystallize in your mind who the character is and what he or she is like. The long-term benefit is that such a paragraph will serve to refresh your memory if the sermon is preached in the future after you have forgotten much of this background material.

After you have gathered and summarized the background material on the character, you need to do one more thing to bring the personality to life. You must mix together exegetical and historical detail with imaginative insight. Without imagination the character lies flat on the page, but if you mix in a little imagination, the character stands up and becomes a flesh-and-blood person.

For example, the story of Naomi in the Book of Ruth is set in the long ago and far away. Yet when you put yourself in the sandals of Naomi, the opening chapter of the Book of Ruth portrays a painfully realistic picture of a woman grieving the loss of a spouse and two sons. Imagine Naomi's grief and feel her pain. If you think about losing the three people closest to you along with all your financial security, you can begin to understand why Naomi was so bitter. You can empathize with her questions: "Why would God let this happen? How could he be so cruel? What good could possibly come from such pain?" Unless you, yourself, feel the sharp edge of Naomi's questions, it is hard to hear God's answer. Until you personally enter into the story, you may never sense the excruciating anguish in the questions she asks.

Imagination therefore is a critical ingredient in preparing to portray the character. However, you must not allow your imagination to run away like a wild stallion. While your imagination is a tool of interpretation, it must be tied to the biblical text. Imagination must be linked to the Scripture passage in the same way interpretation is linked to the text. A preacher needs a healthy imagination, but if the imagination is not guided by the meaning of the text and the historical and cultural setting of the passage, then imagination easily becomes fantasy.

Where Am I?

"Where am I?" is the second critical question you should ask about the character. This question deals with the issue of stance. Stance is the perspective of the character in relation to the twenty-first-century audience. Does the character know the audience? Is the character familiar with our modern culture? In other words, you must ask, "Where is this character in relation to my audience?" Has the character come into the modern world to speak to them or are the listeners transported back to the ancient world of the text? How you answer these questions will determine how you will present your first-person sermon.

There are two stances you may choose to take as a biblical character, each with its own advantages and disadvantages.

1. Transport the Contemporary Audience Back into Ancient Time

You may choose to transport your listeners back in time. With a sanctified use of imagination, you take them back to the period of the judges, the early days of the church, or the very beginning of time. Your audience looks in and listens to the men and women of faith in the world in which they lived. If you choose this stance, you have two options. You may cast your audience as participants in your story and address them directly or you may decide that they will be spectators who look in on the action.

Of these two options, the simplest is to give your audience a part in the story and speak to them directly. For example, in the sermon presented by Sue Robinson as Mary Magdalene (Appendix 6), the listeners are cast as first-century disciples who have yet to hear about Jesus' resurrection. The modern audience becomes Mary Magdalene's ancient audience. She tells her story directly to them. Looking your listeners in the eye and talking to them directly keeps them engaged in what you are saying.

One potential drawback to casting your audience as the ancient audience is that if you're not careful, you will cease to be a storyteller. First-person sermons relate the life experiences of the men and women of Scripture, and people love to hear other people's stories. The strength of narrative is that as you tell the story, your audience lets down their guard to listen. But if a first-person portrayal is too direct, your listeners may become defensive. What they hear is just an old sermon in a thinly veiled disguise.

For a different effect, you may decide to transport your listeners back to the biblical world where they are spectators who eavesdrop on the conversation of the character you portray. From the audience's perspective, this most resembles watching television or watching a play. Fredrick Speakman employs this stance in a sermon where Pilate confesses to an old friend his misgivings about sentencing Jesus to die.[2]

The advantage of indirect address is that it resembles the familiarity of television. Indirect address engages the audience as they overhear the story. The challenge to this stance is that without opportunity to speak directly to your listeners, you must rely on the power of the story and the strength of your portrayal to hold the attention of the audience. This type of first-person sermon is closest to acting. It is difficult to do it well without interpretive training or experience as an actor.

2. Transport the Character into the Modern World

The second possible stance you can take is to "miraculously" resurrect the character and transport him or her into the twenty-first century. This stance often uses flashbacks to the past for telling much of the story.[3] There are two particular strengths to this stance. First, bringing the ancient character into the modern world also allows the character to speak to the audience directly. A second strength of this stance is that it allows the character at least some knowledge of the modern culture. This makes applying biblical truth much easier. Because of these strengths, if you have not done a first-person presentation before, you are likely to feel the most comfortable with this stance.

Before proceeding with your work on the sermon and as you put yourself in the place of the biblical character, it is critical that you ask, "Where am I?" Am I, as the biblical character, to address the audience as contemporaries in my world or am I to travel forward in time to speak to listeners about my experience in their world? For the first-person sermon to stay on track, it is imperative that you make a decision regarding the stance and then remain consistent with that stance throughout the sermon. Inconsistencies in your stance will destroy the effect of a first-person sermon.

Speaking of inconsistencies, anachronism is a common mistake that first-person preachers can easily make. Anachronism is using jargon or references that are out of their proper historical time. For example, Old Testament characters would not have been aware of New Testament texts. Depending on the stance you choose, biblical characters would not have known historical facts about times yet future to their own. It would be inaccurate for Joseph the son of Jacob to say, "My father made sure that we all knew the Ten Commandments." Moses and the Law came almost half a millennium after the time of Joseph.

A clear awareness of the original setting for the story can help you avoid unintended anachronism in your sermon. It is possible, however, to use anachronism intentionally to help your audience hear the old story with new ears. In his sermon on the Book of Ruth (Appendix 1), Steve Mathewson borrows an anachronism from Frederick Buechner to shine some modern light on the ancient story. Ruth 3:10 told it like it was: "'The LORD bless you, my daughter,' [Boaz] replied. 'This kindness is greater than that which you showed earlier: You have not run after younger men, whether rich or poor.'" Mathewson, therefore, also speaks plainly: "Ruth, this act of *HESED* is better than your first act towards your family! You could have run after the young hunks wearing Wranglers. They've been dying to court you."

The stance you choose has practical implications. For one, it will determine the kind of illustrations that are appropriate in the sermon. If the audience is transported back to the ancient world, there can be illustrations, but they are limited. They can only be drawn from the ancient world and must be consistent with the historical and cultural setting of that world and of your character.

For example, in the testimony of Mary Magdalene (Appendix 6), Mary is speaking to followers of Jesus in Galilee shortly after Christ's resurrection. Mary tells those ancient disciples how she had been delivered from the demons that possessed her. She explains, "Now the sunshine seemed to greet me with its warm smile. Now I heard the birds singing and they seemed to be singing to me." It would be anachronistic, not to mention out of character, for Mary to say, "I felt like I had just won the lottery!"

Illustrations are easiest when the ancient character is transported to the modern world and speaks directly to the congregation. We see this clearly in the dialogue between King Herod and the pastor in the sermon on Matthew 2 (Appendix 4). Herod has been allowed to "come back" and speak to a modern audience. The logic that allows for Herod to speak to men and women today assumes that he might also know something about the modern world. Because of this Herod speaks directly to the audience. For instance, when the pastor protests Herod's callousness in the slaughter of innocent babies in Bethlehem because "small children are precious," Herod snaps back, "Are they? Are they really? In your culture you kill over a million of them a year before they are born. You see them wiped out in the streets of your cities or in Belfast or Bosnia or Africa where they starve to death. You go on eating your supper."

The stance you choose will also impact the kind of applications that can be made. Application is simplest when the ancient character is transported to speak to people in the modern world. In Steve Mathewson's sermon on the Book of Ruth, an unnamed elder from Bethlehem travels forward in time more than three thousand years to speak a special word of encouragement to moms on Mother's Day. "The people of God who make the greatest impact do it through ordinary faithfulness."

If you transport the audience back in time so that the character speaks to them in the ancient world, applications are possible but limited. The biblical figure cannot be expected to know anything about life in our day. Any application therefore has to be broad enough to span the centuries. The exhortation of Mary Magdalene to ancient believers in Galilee applies equally today: "Tell everyone, 'Jesus is alive!'"[4]

Summary

An effective first-person sermon requires a character who has a developed personality and who has a clear stance toward the audience. Research mixed together with imagination brings a character to life. A consistent stance determines where the character lives, thereby strengthening the impact of the sermon upon its hearers.

5

Bones and Flesh

Let's review. You have identified your text. Through your exegesis, you have determined the main idea of the passage and researched its characters and setting. You have selected a character and come to grips with the personality of that character. And you have determined the character's stance in relation to the audience. You now have all the raw materials with which to construct a narrative sermon.

Constructing Your Sermon

A sermon is constructed in three stages. First, the preaching idea is stated. Second, the flow of the sermon and its structure are determined. And third, the exegetical background material is used to fill out this structure as the sermon manuscript is written. Let's look at each of these more closely.

Stage 1—State the Sermon's Preaching Idea

No sermon should be preached that hasn't first answered two fundamental questions: What am I saying? And why am I saying it? This first stage of sermon construction gives the sermon its substance and direction. It is here that you identify your preaching idea and your purpose. Sermons that fail at this stage never recover.

To this point in your preparation, the focus has been on understanding the truth of the text. As you begin to prepare your sermon, however, your focus is on communicating that timeless biblical truth to modern listeners. To do that, you must state the exegetical idea in a way that relates to your contemporary audience. This statement is the homiletical or preaching idea. Your preaching idea is your sermon in a nutshell. It is this idea that you will seek to communicate through the sermon.

Here are a few suggestions to help you state the preaching idea:

- State the idea as simply and as memorably as possible. Make each word count. State it for the ear. Listeners should not have to work to remember it.
- State the idea in concrete and familiar words. Study ads in magazines for slogans you remember.
- State the idea so that it focuses on response. How do you want your listeners to respond? If you know what your listeners should do, tell them.
- State the idea so that your listeners sense you are talking *to* them *about* them.

Your character's chosen stance will impact how you state your preaching idea. If the character is brought into the twenty-first century, the idea may be directly stated in relation to your modern audience. The character speaking directly to today's listeners might say, "Even in hospital rooms and funeral homes, you can be sure of God's presence." If the audience is transported back into ancient times, the idea may have to be stated more broadly: "Even in your most painful moments and even when you stand by a grave, God will never leave you nor forsake you." Occasionally, it is possible for the idea to be a clear statement of the exegetical idea, but it is always best to state the idea so that it effectively addresses the needs of the modern audience without being anachronistic to an ancient setting.

Stage 2—Determine the Purpose of Your Sermon

As you begin thinking about your sermon's preaching idea, you must also determine your purpose. The homiletical idea is the substance of what you want the sermon to say. Your purpose describes what you want the sermon to do. Why are you preaching this message? In other words, how do you want people to respond?[1]

Specifically, how might your listeners apply the truth of the text to their lives in the week ahead? Direct application can be difficult in a first-person sermon. That is all the more reason why you must clarify for yourself what that application should be. For instance, the Galatians sermon (Appendix 7) was preached on Easter Sunday. Two purposes guided the sermon. The primary purpose of the sermon was to clearly communicate the good news of Jesus to seekers who inevitably swell church attendance on Easter. The secondary purpose for the sermon was to introduce a sermon series from Galatians. It was hoped that this first-person sermon might entice visitors to come back and hear more. As you read through the sermon, you can see how these two purposes shaped the message. The primary purpose directed the sermon to the application summed up in the last words of the sermon: "Let go."

Stage 3—Determine the Structure and Flow of the Sermon

Once you have clearly stated the idea of the passage in terms of the audience and determined what you expect them to do in response to your sermon, you are ready for stage 3. This third phase in the construction of a first-person sermon builds a structure for the story that will be told by your character. There are two things you need to do at this stage: Put down the skeleton events of the story and decide how you will tell those events to clearly develop the central idea.

Map out the structure of the original story. If the biblical passage is drawn from nonnarrative material, you'll want to sketch out the structure of the story that relates to the text. For example, if you were preaching a first-person sermon as an overview to Paul's second letter to Timothy, this letter (like every letter) has a story that surrounds it. Paul had apparently won Timothy to Christ in Lystra and later invited him to join the apostle on his missionary travels. After release from his first imprisonment in Rome, Paul left Timothy in Ephesus to straighten out problems there. Now, at the end of his ministry, Paul is once again imprisoned in Rome and he senses that the end is near. From the loneliness of a dungeon Paul writes Timothy to give him some final instructions and to ask Timothy to come visit him in prison. This history forms the background to the text of 2 Timothy. As with narrative literature, this story can be broken down into parts.

This process of dividing up the narrative might be conceived of as scenes in a movie or play. The story surrounding 2 Timothy might be broken into three scenes: scene 1—Paul's history with Timothy; scene 2—Paul's instruction to Timothy (in this letter); and scene 3—his final words to Timothy.

In narrative literature, this process is usually much simpler. In the Book of Ruth, for example, the action can easily be broken down into four scenes. Each chapter of the book depicts a different scene. In scene 1, Naomi returns to Bethlehem with her daughter-in-law Ruth, having lost to death her husband and two sons. In the second scene, Boaz and Ruth meet in the harvest fields. Scene 3 depicts Ruth's proposal to Boaz at the threshing floor. In the fourth scene, Boaz settles matters with his kinsman at the city gate, and the story comes to a satisfying conclusion.[2]

Once you have determined the structure of the passage, you are ready to craft the structure of your first-person sermon. This necessitates a bit of creativity. You cannot retell the biblical story exactly as it was recorded. That would be redundant. Your task is to tell the same story but in an imaginative way that effectively communicates the preaching idea to your audience.

Decide how you will tell those events to clearly develop the central idea. There are various structures available to help you effectively communicate the story's idea to your listeners. For instance, you may choose to employ either a chronological, psychological, or dramatic structure.

Chronological Structure—the story can be developed chronologically to parallel the way the events actually occurred. Chronological structure, as the name suggests, follows a sequence of time. The events in the story are retold in the order they happened. In telling someone's life story, selected events would be described as they happened in that person's life. Sid Buzzel's sermon on Proverbs 4:23 (Appendix 3) is structured for the most part chronologically. It begins in the present by talking about a letter received from an old classmate. News from the letter leads to a flashback to the storyteller's college days. From that point on the story unfolds chronologically, one event after another to the end of the story. Although this structure is usually clear and easy to follow, it is often more difficult to provide the sermon with a strong climax.

Psychological Structure—the story can be developed psychologically, starting at the conclusion and showing how you got there. To tighten the climactic strings of a story, a psychological structure may prove helpful. This structure makes use of flashback to retell earlier episodes in the character's life. However, these episodes are not necessarily retold in the order they would have occurred but in the way they stand out in the character's mind. In retelling the story psychologically, the character employs flashback and skips around in time.

Kent Edwards's sermon on 1 Samuel (Appendix 2) is structured psychologically. The events of the story are arranged to reveal the answer to the question raised in the sermon's introduction, "What makes a leader?" In the introduction Edwards raises the question, "What does it mean to be a leader?" Then he assumes the role of Eliab, King David's older brother, who tells the story. Eliab begins by relating a pivotal incident in his life. As the oldest of Jesse's sons, Eliab was sure he would be anointed as king, but the prophet Samuel chose David instead. Eliab's musing as to why David was selected as leader causes the storyteller to reflect back to an earlier incident. In David's battle with Goliath, Eliab and his listeners finally learn what makes a leader. Eliab's search for an answer shapes the psychological development of the sermon.

Dramatic Structure—the story can be developed in a dramatic form, similar to that of a play. Sermons arranged according to a dramatic structure provide the answer to three questions. According to Harold Freeman:

> The drama begins by answering the question, What is going on here? which produces clear statements describing the situation

> in all its various dimensions. Next, the drama continues by addressing the question, What are the ramifications of this situation? That is, the complications of the situation are portrayed in a way designed to arouse suspense concerning its outcome. At the end the story answers the question, How did it turn out?[3]

Whatever the stance, whether the character flashes back to the past or the audience is transported back in time, from that point on the dramatic structure unfolds like a play.

The sermon on the Book of Ruth (Appendix 1) follows both a chronological and a dramatic structure because the Book of Ruth unfolds both chronologically and dramatically. Primarily, however, the Book of Ruth is structured like a play. In chapter 1 Naomi and Ruth get into trouble. In chapter 2 we begin to see a ray of hope for Ruth and her mother-in-law. Chapter 3 adds a couple of wrinkles that must be ironed out. And in the last scene, chapter 4, the conflict is resolved. Naomi is provided for and Ruth gets a husband. Steve Mathewson organized his sermon to fit the dramatic structure of the book.

At this point, you have determined the sermon's structure and flow. You know the basic shape the sermon will take and how the action will be brought to climax and then resolution. These are the bones of the sermon. But you can't let a sermon run around in its bones. Now you must put meat on the skeleton.

Stage 4—Fill in the Exegetical and Historical Details of the Sermon As You Write out the Sermon Manuscript

Skeletons are rather unattractive. It is the muscle and skin hanging on them that make them appealing. The historical, geographical, and cultural material you have uncovered in your exegesis fleshes out the bones of your structure. Use this exegetical material to fill out each scene as you write the sermon manuscript. Describe the locale. Is it in the country or the city, in the mountains or by the shore? What do you see? How does it smell? What sounds do you hear? Picture the characters in each scene. How do they look, act, and talk? As you add the historical and cultural details to each scene, the skeleton will get up and walk around.

While other aspects of preparing a first-person sermon are more demanding than a traditional sermon, writing the sermon manuscript is usually easier. Once the biblical story has been analyzed, the exegetical details have been gathered, and the structure and flow of the sermon determined, the first-person sermon almost writes itself.[4] Your background study will also make the sermon easier to keep in mind when it is preached.[5]

Write your manuscript in conversational language using short sentences, even contractions and fragments. Use active verbs and concrete nouns. A good practice to help develop oral style is to say the sentence out loud before you write it.

Kent Edwards's sermon on 1 Samuel (Appendix 2) is a great example of oral style. It is neither polished nor formal, but it fits the style of someone sharing his experiences:

> Goliath steps forward. He stands in front of his army and us, and he defies the armies of God. Goliath yells to us, "You servants of Saul. Why should we all fight? Just send one man, if you have one, to come and do battle with me. And if he beats me and kills me, we all will serve you. But if I defeat him and kill him, then you will all serve me. Come send a man, send a man."
>
> Well, none of us really felt like going right then. We were busy. You know, we had things to do. Get ready for battle, all that kind of stuff.
>
> Next morning came. Saul had to do something. So we got ready for battle. All the preparations were made. We got together and he gave us the pep talk. We were getting ready for the battle. And we all ended with the war cry, getting ready for the charge down the hill to meet the Philistines. . . . RUAHH! RUAHH! We were ready! RUAHH! We started down the hill and Goliath walked up. Ruahh!? . . . oohah . . . "You know," we reasoned, "anyone thought of lunch? I'm ready to, you know, take a break." And we walked back.[6]

Introductions and conclusions present unique challenges in a first-person sermon. Your choice of stance or costume will impact your introduction and conclusion. The introduction must introduce, not just the sermon, but also the character. If you are not dressed in costume, it is important that you establish your character early on so that the audience will understand that you have taken on a different persona. If you begin in costume, without prior introduction, listeners may be a bit uneasy until the bearded character in first-century dress introduces himself as the apostle Paul.

If you wear an elaborate costume, you may want to have someone else introduce you before you step out on stage. Or you may choose to begin the sermon in the first person and quickly introduce yourself as the biblical character.[7] However you do it, near the outset it is important that the audience understand who you are as the biblical character.

If you do not wear a costume, you may choose to begin the sermon in the third person as yourself and then step into the first-person role as you introduce the character.[8] You might say to the audience: "Have you ever wondered what it must have been like to have spent time with Jesus, to see him calm raging storms and watch him heal the deathly ill? Well today, we are privileged to have with us a man who was there. His name is Simon Peter. [*Looking to the side*]: Should we call you Simon or Peter?" [*Then stepping to the side and looking back where you had been standing, begin as Peter*]: "Well my parents named me Simon, but I always liked Peter. You know how I got that name, don't you? . . ."

Because a first-person sermon tells a story, you don't want to give away your preaching idea in the introduction. Stories are inductive. The idea of your sermon, therefore, should usually emerge toward the end rather than the beginning of your message.

The introduction should raise a question or create some sort of tension that will have to be answered or resolved in the remainder of the sermon. It is this tension that gives energy to a first-person sermon.

Conclusions present two challenges. First, how do you step out of your character? Second, how do you apply the sermon? The first challenge has only two answers. You either end the sermon as the character or you end it as yourself. If you are wearing an elaborate costume, it is generally best to conclude the sermon in character and step off the stage. If you have no costume or if your costume is easily removed, you may step out of character and end the sermon as yourself. This allows you as the preacher to make a direct application of the sermon when such an application is not possible as the character.

With or without costume, however, once you step out of character and return to "plain old you," your audience's interest will quickly wane. Here are two suggestions to keep in mind. The first and most advisable is: be brief. When you step out of character, you will do well to bring your sermon to a quick conclusion, while you still hold your listeners' attention.

Depending on your stance, it can be difficult to make a direct application to your audience. For that reason, you may find that you still have some important things to say after you step out of character. If so, to keep your audience on track with you, you must move from the biblical character's story to another story. Don't expect your audience to make the trip with you from the concrete images in a story to abstract statements of truth. Some listeners may follow you but not many and not for long.

You need to move from the biblical story to one that helps your listeners apply the truth from Scripture to their lives. The sermon on Galatians 1–2 (Appendix 7) demonstrates that move. It begins with Paul's story, which makes the point that salvation is a matter of God's grace that we must trust. The sermon concludes with an anecdote to encourage each listener to trust God. Just remember, if there is more to be said after the biblical character has spoken, keep it brief or tell a story of your own.

The challenge of making direct application depends on your stance. It is easiest to apply your idea directly when you transport your character forward in time to speak directly to your audience. When you take the audience back to listen to your character in the ancient world, your primary obstacle is anachronism. While you can warn your listeners to stay away from the seductress, you cannot warn your audience to stay away from pornography on the Internet. If the sermon is a reenactment of a story from the ancient world, the simplest way to make direct application is to conclude the reenactment and then make the application directly as yourself.

Although this may be the easiest, it is not necessarily the most effective. The power of the first-person sermon resembles the impact of a play. Watching a play in a theater moves and changes us because the power of the drama lies in the interaction between the characters and what we bring to the play, not in a specific application made to our lives. At the end of the play, the director seldom steps out in front of the curtain to explain to the audience what we have seen. The drama itself has conveyed the message.[9]

Summary

Preparation for a first-person narrative sermon requires that you take your exegetical odds and ends and transform them into a unified, well-written expository sermon manuscript. You begin by stating your preaching idea and your purpose. Next you give the sermon flow and structure. Then you mix in the fruits of your exegesis as you write out your sermon.

When the last of these stages is complete, you have a sermon—on paper. But you're not done just yet. Sermons are not books. They are presented live and in person.

6

It's All in How You Tell It

It was John's first day in prison. Mike, the prisoner in the adjoining cell, had obviously been in for a while. As John sat in his cell thinking about the long months ahead, he heard Mike yell out, "Thirty-one!" In response, all the men in the nearby cells rolled off their beds with laughter. When the laughter had subsided, Mike bellowed out once again, "Seventeen!" Again laughter rang out throughout the cell block.

After a while, John had to know why everyone would laugh when Mike called out a number. Mike explained, "You see, we've been in this place so long, we've heard every joke at least a hundred times. So, since we already know all the jokes, instead of telling the same jokes over and over again, we just give every joke a number, and it saves the time and energy of retelling the same old stories."

"All right," said John, "let me try." John called out at the top of his voice, "Number three!" This time, however, no one uttered a sound. John raised his voice again. "Number three!" he yelled. Still, no response.

"Hey man, what gives?" John asked Mike. "How come when you call out a number, everyone laughs, but when I do it, nobody even smiles?"

"Well, John," replied Mike, "some folks know how to tell a joke, and some just don't."

In first-person preaching, as in comedy, delivery is critical. If you fail to present your sermon well, all the study, writing, and hard work to this point will be of little value. The techniques involved in delivering a first-person sermon are not difficult to master, but even seasoned preachers may not be familiar with the staging and delivery required of an effective presentation.

Some of these techniques come from the field of drama rather than homiletics. There is much that preachers can learn from the actor's craft. Twenty-first-century preachers are not the first to recognize this: "Cicero, like Demosthenes before him, belonged to a long line of famous orators who learned effective public delivery by studying actors."[1] Even if you never preach a first-person sermon, your sermons will benefit from an awareness of the actor's techniques.

There are three tools available to the first-person preacher, drawn from the fields of both drama and homiletics, that will enhance the presentation of your sermon. They are physical movement, delivery, and costuming. A knowledge of these tools and how best to use them can make your sermon more effective.

1. Physical Movement

Experts tell us that up to 93 percent of the messages we communicate are nonverbal.[2] That means that what we say accounts for less than one tenth of the message we convey to others. Our verbal inflection, eye contact, and body movements speak even when we aren't talking. While all aspects of nonverbal communication are associated with delivery, one nonverbal cue—movement—is worth special mention.

Students of drama understand the importance of movement. In rehearsal, actors block every scene to determine where each character will be positioned and what their movements will be. While first-person preaching is not acting, when preaching any kind of sermon—traditional or first-person—your movements communicate. Whether they communicate what you want them to say is determined to some degree by your understanding of movement.

As one expert says, "Do not do anything 'in general.' 'In general' is the enemy of art."[3] General movement is ineffective. Movement without purpose and thought may hinder rather than help communication. Plan your movement before you preach.

The following is a diagram of the platform or stage area where you will deliver your first-person sermon.

Audience		
Area 4 Cool Distress, Conflict	**Area 1** Medium Confrontational	**Area 3** Warm Intimate
Area 6 Cold Extreme Alienation	**Area 2** Medium Distant, Aloof	**Area 5** Warm More Distant

Notice that each block has different words that describe it. Reg Grant and John Reed explain: "The psychology of aesthetics tells us that audiences respond instinctively and uniquely to each area of the stage. . . . They perceive each block as relatively 'strong' or 'weak,' 'cool' or 'warm.' You can assign the scenes of your story to each accordingly.

"The six areas are numbered in order of 'strength.' As a general rule, the closer you are to your audience, the stronger the impression you will make. The farther away you are, the more remote you will seem. As you face the audience, scenes played to your right (stage right) will tend to be warmer emotionally, while scenes played to your left (stage left) will tend to be cooler."[4]

As you read through your sermon manuscript, determine where you will position yourself in each scene. You want your placement on the stage to support what you are saying. Being intentional about blocking each scene, associating your message with your physical movements, can aid you in keeping your sermon in mind.

2. Delivery

Delivery consists of more than a single tool. It resembles a toolbox containing both the verbal and nonverbal skills you use to communicate. A few aspects of delivery are particularly important to first-person sermons.

A first-person sermon must be delivered without notes. This is true for several reasons. First, notes hinder effective communication. This is true regardless of the sermon form. In fact, if preaching first-person sermons weans you away from using notes in your other sermons, your preaching will profit from it.

Second, although we have been calling this presentation a sermon, actually it resembles a one-sided conversation. It is best to step away from the pulpit when doing a first-person sermon; better still, remove the pulpit all together.

Using notes is more than just awkward. They are inauthentic to the message you are communicating. In this one-sided conversation, the character you are portraying is sharing personal experiences. None of us reads note cards when we talk with a friend about growing up, about a conflict we had at the office, or about an accident that crippled us. Those events are embedded in our memories. They are part of what makes us who we are. We don't need notes when we tell our memories. It would be silly therefore to expect Joshua to use notes as he described his battle at Jericho. Peter wouldn't use notes in recounting his experience of seeing Jesus alive after he came back from the grave.

All this is to say, ***NO NOTES ALLOWED!!!*** But don't panic. There is good news: first-person sermons remember themselves. If you have followed all the steps in planning and writing your sermon, you probably already have a rough draft of the sermon in your head.

Preaching without notes does not require that you memorize your manuscript. In fact, memorizing the manuscript has at least two disadvantages. First, memorization is simply too much work. If you feel that you must memorize your manuscript every time you preach a first-person sermon, you won't preach them very often. Who has time to regularly memorize a twenty-five-minute monologue.

Moreover, a first-person sermon is more authentic if it is relived rather than recited. If Joshua were describing the battle of Jericho, he wouldn't recite chapters 5 and 6 of Joshua from memory. He'd retell the story as he relived it. If Peter were speaking about Christ's murder and resurrection, he wouldn't recite the events like a creed. With shame and embarrassment he would recall his cowardice and betrayal. And he would shed tears of joy at his restoration. That's reliving the event. No one recites vital life experiences from memory.

If you must memorize something, then memorize the structure of your sermon. You will need to keep in mind its various movements. If you've done your exegesis, you will have plenty of material to paint each scene for your audience. See it in your mind and then describe it. Although you don't memorize the entire sermon, you might find it helpful to memorize the introduction and conclusion. At the moment you step up to begin your sermon, you may feel a twinge of stage fright. A memorized introduction may help give you greater confidence. And having the conclusion memorized gives you the assurance that you'll land the sermon safely.

If you are going to be intentional in your movement and confident in your delivery, then some rehearsal is essential. It is important that you talk through the entire sermon without your manuscript at least once before you preach. In addition, it can be beneficial if you can not only think through the structure of your sermon but, as you do, walk through it on the platform where you plan to preach. If that is not possible, then picture the stage in your mind and imagine where you will position yourself as you talk through the sermon.

Eye contact is important in the delivery of any sermon. Appropriate eye contact will depend on the stance you choose for the character. If your stance allows the character to speak directly to the audience, look your listeners in the eyes as you speak. This helps hold their attention and enables you to know whether you're connecting with them.

If you decide to transport your audience back into the ancient world where they observe your biblical character interacting with other individuals in the story, you will benefit from a few interpretive techniques. First, decide whether to address your audience directly or indirectly. If you choose to speak directly, then establish eye contact with different listeners as you speak. If your character is reflecting on a past memory, or feeling introspective, use less direct eye contact with your listeners. We do that in ordinary conversation, and your ancient character is having an ordinary conversation with folks in your audience.

If you choose not to speak directly to your audience, avoid making eye contact with your listeners. Instead, look slightly over their heads. Do not focus on objects on the platform. When you do this, you direct your listeners' attention to the rostrum, and this limits their imaginative participation. Avoid staring at the ground. This causes the audience to establish the scene on the ground. Because your listeners see the scene largely through your facial expression, try not to turn too much to either side. If your audience cannot see your face, they cannot see the scene.

Your focus is where you look. With your eyes, place other imagined characters out in front of you. If you interact with only one character, establish your focus directly in front of you and slightly above the heads of your audience. If the imaginary character is to the left, when you address him, you need to look slightly to the left. If he is taller than you, look up when you speak to him. This helps your audience visualize the character as you speak.

If you speak to more than one person, use your focus to give each of the other characters a permanent placement. As you address other characters, however, feel free to let your focus wander from that fixed spot as you do in normal conversation. In general, place the most important character in the center and other characters to the left and right of the major character.[5]

Don't try to act, just tell the story through your character's eyes. Eye contact, movement, and gestures will all be more natural if you *relive* the story rather than *retell* it. Put yourself in the sandals of the character. See each scene as the character sees it. Feel what the character feels. Let your vocal and physical response come from within and be appropriate to the character you are presenting.

3. Costuming

Like delivery, costuming is more than a single tool. It too is a box containing *costume, makeup,* and *props*. Each of these can greatly enhance the presentation of your message. At the same time, each has its own drawbacks.

A *costume* can aid in the portrayal of a character. A good costume always fits. First, it fits the historical setting. It accurately represents the clothing worn during the time period depicted in the drama. Second, a good costume fits the actor. It is neither too large nor too small. Third, a good costume fits the role of the character, strengthening the role without calling attention to itself.

A well-conceived costume benefits both you and your audience. You benefit because a good costume helps you assume the character. We experience this power of costume every day. The Little League baseball team plays better once their uniforms arrive. When you come home from work, you get out of your work clothes and slip into casual apparel. On the weekend, you plan a special night out, so you dress in a tuxedo or an evening gown. You feel elegant because you dress elegantly. You buy a new suit and exclaim, "I feel like a new person." The old cliché "Clothes make the man" is on to something. The fact is, what you wear often affects your perception of yourself. A costume helps to create the character.

That is true both for yourself and for your audience. The costume that helps you assume the character also helps your listeners assume that you are the character. When you sign the thirty-year mortgage on a new house, you have more confidence in an attorney wearing a three-piece suit than one dressed in cutoffs and a sweat-stained T-shirt. You assess their competencies based not on the law school from which they graduated or the grades they received but on their "costume." One looks professional and the other doesn't.

Non-actors may decide that they don't need a costume when preaching a first-person sermon. After all, the pulpit isn't theater. Yet perhaps that betrays how much we underestimate the power of costume. Jac and Miriam Lewis put a different spin on our thinking: "An actor who avoids disguise is himself playing a role, relying upon his own physical aspects or personal magnetism."[6]

Although a costume can be a great help to you as you preach a first-person sermon, it can also get in the way. A costume can be so overpowering that it distracts from and diminishes your portrayal. For instance, your costume could prove to be unsuitable to the role. It may be so big that you stumble over it or so small that you can't move freely, or be of such poor quality that it distracts your listeners. You will not help them by wearing a bathrobe or a bedsheet or by talking to them about the things of God with a beard that looks like a cotton ball hanging from the end of your chin. Such costumes only make it harder for people to listen.

Experienced actors know the hazards of bad costumes:

> For good or evil, the costume's influence upon the actor is enormous. There have been many disasters impressed upon helpless performers by unintelligent costuming and, no matter how hard they try, the acting is made either ridiculous or subservient to the costume.[7]

Here are two important guidelines to help you decide whether to use a costume. First, use a costume if it helps you assume the character and if it will make the character more believable to the audience. Ask yourself, "Will wearing a costume benefit my listeners?" Second, use a costume if you can do so given the constraints of your facility and your time. If there is not adequate time in the service or program for you to change into your costume, then don't use it. If you need a sink, a mirror, or a changing room for the costume and none is available, save the costume for another time.

A costume is a powerful tool that enhances the effectiveness of a first-person sermon. If you are confident that you can make use of a costume to the benefit of your audience, you will be glad you did. But if you are unsure of the wisdom of employing a costume for the sermon, follow this advice gained from hard experience: if in doubt, do without.

Along with costumes, a second tool available to you as you plan your presentation is *makeup*. There are two reasons to consider using makeup. Makeup has long been used in the theater to compensate for inadequate lighting. Although the lighting in some churches might make the use of makeup advisable, this is not your basic concern. Its primary benefit is that it enhances your costume: "Makeup has the ability to immediately define age, health, sex, race, traits, manner and profession of the character."[8] Makeup can be used to age your character or to achieve historical accuracy with beards, mustaches, and hairstyles of the ancient world.

While makeup can be employed to great advantage, overusing makeup is the mark of an amateur. Makeup is best used only when necessary to achieve a particular effect and with as much discretion as possible.

Costume and makeup can help reveal at least seven features of your character's physical image: genetics, environment, health, disfigurements, fashion, personality, and age.[9]

In addition to costumes and makeup, *props* are a third tool at your disposal. "Props" is short for properties and refers to the moveable articles on the platform, which are used to aid your presentation. Props can be used with a costume to strengthen its impact. What would Moses be without a staff, little David without his slingshot, or Pilate without a washbasin? Careful thought should be given to any props you might use. Unnecessary props are an encumbrance and can easily become a distraction to you and to your listeners. If you use a prop, be sure to rehearse using it so that you are comfortable with it.

Props can be used to suggest a costume. One prop utilized in different ways can distinguish different characters. A simple shawl worn over the head, over the shoulders, or tied around the waist could suggest the priest, the Levite, and the Samaritan who happened upon a mugging victim on the highway to Jericho.

Costumes, makeup, and props all deserve consideration in your presentation of a first-person sermon. Used wisely, they have the potential to make a memorable sermon unforgettable.

First-Person Presentation Checklist

The following checklist may help you as you prepare for the presentation of your first-person sermon:

1. Use the material from your exegesis to form a mental picture of your character. Consider again the following characteristics about the character:

- placement in time
- ethnic background
- social position
- economic standing
- home environment

2. After you have determined the identifying background, begin your detective work to find a visual model for your character. This is worth doing even if you don't plan to use a costume. Clothing is the clue. Begin your search for:

   - clothing style of the culture and time period
   - style of clothing the character wears in relation to his position in life
   - type of fabric and choice of color you envision as suitable to the role
   - posture of individual with respect to his clothing and status

   Sources for research:

   - Bible handbooks and encyclopedias
   - libraries—books on costume and makeup may prove helpful[10]
   - movies
   - television

3. Design, buy, or rent a costume that fits what you have learned about the character. (At this time you may decide merely to use a prop without a costume, or you may choose not to use a prop or costume at all.) Make sure the costume is not unnecessarily restrictive or uncomfortable.
4. Decide on your hairstyle and facial appearance including the use of any makeup.
5. Rehearse with your costume (and/or accessories) and makeup.

7

Curing First-Person Headaches

Headaches can be annoying. Migraine headaches can be incapacitating. The throbbing in your head can force you to stop doing what you're doing. Headaches can cause you to quit. Some require codeine to help you function again.

Anyone who has ever seriously considered first-person preaching knows that there are unique challenges associated with this kind of expository sermon. Some of these challenges, like headaches, may tempt you to quit before you ever begin.

None of the challenges to first-person preaching, however, are insurmountable. The problems have solutions. The headaches have cures.

The following are some of the most commonly asked questions about preaching first-person sermons.

Is the First-Person Preaching Form Biblical?

The shortest answer to that question is no and yes. No, there is no right sermon form prescribed in the Bible. Traditional sermons are no more biblical than newer forms. The deductive sermon form, the primary model of sermons for centuries, derives not from the Bible but from Greco-Roman rhetoric. The Bible does not require that sermons come in any one size or shape. There is no eleventh commandment that mandates "Thou shalt preach first-person sermons and preach them only." But then again, there is no eleventh commandment about any sermon form.

But yes, first-person preaching is at the same time quite biblical. At their essence, first-person sermons are narratives, and narrative is the dominant literary form in Scripture: "Over 40 percent of the Old Testament is narrative," and "the Old Testament constitutes three-quarters of the bulk of the Bible."[1] While most biblical narrative is told in the third person, there are numerous examples of first-person narrative in the Bible. Examples include Daniel 4, Nehemiah, and the "we" sections in Acts; in addition there is plenty of first-person material tucked away in third-person narrative as well as other literary genres. Examples include Joshua 14, Psalm 73, and the Book of Revelation. The letters of Paul are all written from his first-person perspective. While there is no one right sermon form, first-person sermons fit the genre of much of the Bible.

First-person preaching isn't the only way to preach or even the most commonly used method. Scripture itself comes in a variety of genres. To some degree, biblical sermons should reflect the literature from which they are drawn. In many instances, first-person sermons do that best.

Can Anyone, Including Non-actors, Preach a First-Person Sermon?

The fact is, anyone can preach a first-person sermon and preach it effectively. You need not be a skilled actor to preach a first-person sermon. Competent preachers who follow the suggestions given in this book will be able to construct and deliver a good first-person expository sermon.

You do not need dramatic training or great skill as an actor to preach a first-person sermon. The delivery of a first-person sermon isn't so much about acting as it is the ability to tell a biblical character's story from his or her point of view. Some will, no doubt, be better at it than others. Some will be drawn to it more than others. You'll never know how well you can present a first-person sermon until you try one.

Other preachers may be put off by the thought of preaching a sermon without notes. But you will be a more effective communicator if you learn to be note-free, whatever your sermon form.

When Do I Use a Costume?

Although this question has already been addressed, it may be worth further elaboration. The answer in the previous chapter had two parts. First, use a costume only if it will help your audience more fully enter into your portrayal as the character. Seldom will this not be the case. A good costume almost always enhances your characterization. Ideally, most first-person sermons would be done in costume.

Nevertheless, costumes do add an extra element of work to a sermon form that is already labor-intensive. Your limited preparation time will often prohibit use of an elaborate costume. Add to that the time constraints of the preaching service and limitations of the facility to allow you to change into the costume, and it may prove unwise, even disastrous to wear an elaborate costume.

But this is not the end of the matter. Seldom do you have to choose between an elaborate costume or no costume. It may be possible to simplify your costume. Instead of dying your hair and gluing on a beard, you can slip into a tunic. If elaborate costumes are not possible there are often simpler alternatives.

Ways to simplify your costume are limited only by your inventiveness and good judgment. Ruth might be suggested by wearing a shawl. Joseph in the Old Testament could wear a multicolored robe. Peter might wear blue jeans and a T-shirt that says "I'd rather be fishing."

If even a simple costume won't work, a prop might do. All Moses needs is a staff; the woman at the well, a wooden bucket; Stephen, a stone. Creativity and excellence are key. Doing without a costume or prop is always preferable to outfitting your character in a shoddy manner.

Since This Is Exposition, How Do I Point Out the Text to My Audience?

Good question! Keeping listeners mindful of the biblical text is not a simple task. You do, however, have a few options. The best choice will vary from sermon to sermon.

You may choose to read the text before the sermon. This helps your listeners recognize that the sermon is based on the Bible, not your imagination. Some texts seem to raise more questions than offer answers. If your sermon addresses some of those questions, reading the passage before you preach might be the best approach.

Sometimes, however, reading the text before you preach risks giving away the tension of your sermon. In that case, it is best not to do so.[2]

Another option is to read (or ask someone else to read) the passage after you preach. If your listeners are not aware that the story you are telling comes from Scripture, read the text after you preach and people will see it with new eyes. For instance, in the introduction to your sermon, identify yourself as a worship leader. In the sermon, confess the difference that worship made to you at a time when you almost lost your faith, then at the conclusion, read Psalm 73. Your listeners will realize that the problem that brought you to the edge of despair was actually the experience of the psalmist.

You may opt to refer to the text as you preach. This is most easily done when you begin as yourself. Before stepping into the portrayal of your character, you may choose to read the text or ask your listeners to turn to the passage and follow along. Kent Edwards does this well in the introduction to his sermon from 1 Samuel 16–17 (Appendix 2).

In some cases the character himself may refer the listeners to the biblical text. In the sample sermon from Galatians 1–2 (Appendix 7), the apostle Paul directly speaks about the significance of the opening verses of his letter to the Galatians.

Your authority as a preacher rests on the Scripture from which you preach. Your listeners will be well served if you do your best to keep them mindful of the text.

How Do I Differentiate between Biblical Fact and My Own Interpretation in a First-Person Sermon?

Any sermon in any form is susceptible to faulty interpretation of the Scripture. Truth and interpretation, history and imagination are woven into every sermon. The question in the first-person sermon is this: When you know you are engaging in speculative interpretation, or speculative imagination, is there a way to differentiate the *most likely* from the *given?*

The best remedy for this is careful exegesis. It is a sin to say "in God's name" what he never intended. As an expository preacher, the message you deliver should be the product of diligent study and research. To the best of your ability, you should endeavor to accurately understand and communicate the Scriptures. This will not eliminate faulty interpretations or baseless imagination. It is, however, an important first step.

If you have to make an uncertain judgment call on a text and your conscience demands that you give a specific disclaimer about your sermon, that isn't hard to accommodate. Kent Edwards has a specific suggestion that is worth applying to all debatable exegetical calls:

> When it is necessary to use "sanctified imagination" in recreating an event, I always announce in my prologue that while not all of the information presented comes directly from the pages of Scripture, every detail has been thoroughly researched and is historically, culturally, and socially consistent with that day.[3]

Paul's words to the Corinthians describe our situation: "I know in part" (1 Cor. 13:12). We won't always make the right calls. But careful study and candor with our listeners are two important safeguards.

How Often Should I Use First-Person Sermons for the Method to Remain Effective?

The first time you preach a first-person sermon to a congregation be prepared for an enthusiastic response, assuming you do a good job, of course. Some of that response will be due to the novelty of this sermon form. It is fresh and unusual, and people can easily get excited about it.

By the time you've preached your third or fourth first-person sermon, people will become more accustomed to them. Preach many first-person sermons, and people may no longer respond to them as a novel approach to the biblical text.

But don't confuse novelty with effectiveness. Traditional sermons have been preached for centuries. They ceased being novel long before any of us ever heard our first sermon. Nevertheless, most of us have heard many effective traditional sermons.

The novelty of first-person expository sermons will wane, but the effectiveness of this form for our current generation is virtually guaranteed. The narrative aspect of first-person sermons gives them the ring of relevance to a culture influenced by the power of story.

Given their effectiveness, you are wise to use them often. Then look for new ways to make use of them. Use first-person to add zest to a didactic sermon. For example, in a sermon on 2 Timothy 4, you might combine first-person insights to help communicate Paul's final instructions to Timothy. It might sound something like this:

> Sometimes the words of Paul's New Testament letters seem rather dry and academic. I suppose we could dissect these verses to find three or four things for us to do and file them away in our notebooks. We might be able to suck out the substance of these verses, but we would then miss their spirit.
>
> We cannot appreciate what Paul says until we think about why he says it. Paul is in prison, alone except for Luke, the physician who was with him to the end. Now he pens these words to Timothy, perhaps the last words he ever wrote. What do you think was going on in Paul's mind? From these verses before us, we can imagine Paul's conversation with Luke. As he thinks about what he will write, Paul might have said, "Luke, I am almost through with this letter I've been writing to Timothy. It's a good thing too because from what the guards are saying, I don't suspect I'll get out of this prison. Emperor Nero doesn't have much of a soft spot in his heart for Christians. . . .
>
> "My, this time of year it can get so cold in this place. The chill goes right through me. If fall is this nippy, I hate to think what

winter will be like. I wish I had the cloak I left back in Troas with Carpus. . . ."

"Yes, that's a good idea, Luke. I'll ask Timothy to bring it. I do hope he can get here soon. If the cold doesn't get me, Nero likely will. . . ."

A first-person perspective can add flavor to a third-person narrative sermon as well. Years ago, John Hercus modeled this for us in his retelling of the story of Jacob and Rachel. Notice how he injects Jacob's first-person account into this third-person narrative:

> This is what we read in the case-notes God has left us in the Book of Genesis: "So Jacob served seven years for Rachel, and they seemed to him but a few days because of the love he had for her."
>
> Jacob is in love. Madly, passionately in love. Probably for the first time in all his young life, he has begun to feel the deep emotional security of being rated, of being himself. He is working for Rachel. He is going to be married, married to Rachel:
>
> > "You know Rachel, don't you? She's that lovely, beautiful girl over there. And she's not only the prettiest girl in the world, she's a wonder with the flocks, and very nice to talk to, and quick, and intelligent, and a great girl in the home, and just the most gorgeous looking girl you ever saw, and, and . . . I am going to marry her. Yes. Only seven years . . ."
> >
> > "Gee—it's only three years off. . . ."
> >
> > "Gosh—next year I'm going to be married to Rachel. . . ."
> >
> > "Hey—wake up fellahs, it'll be dawn soon. And today I'm getting married to Rachel. Aren't I just the luckiest dog in the world? Rachel! Married to Rachel! Hurrah, today—Rachel!"
>
> Yes. It's the wedding day. The seven years were nothing to Jacob, so long as he married lovely Rachel. And the ceremony is in progress. . . . [4]

The combination of a first-person movement within a third-person narrative sermon allows you both to witness the story and enter into it. Combining these two narrative forms is another way to keep a new form fresh.

However you use it, long after first-person preaching ceases to be novel, it will continue to be effective. Someday it will no longer be a new form, but it can become an old friend.

Introduction to the Appendices

The following appendices are intended to accompany the material in the book. Each of the first seven appendices contains the manuscript of a first-person expository sermon. As written examples, they cannot fully convey the dynamic, emotion, and impact of the sermons as actually delivered.

A first-person sermon manuscript is not so much a script as it is a guide. Consequently, the wording and possibly the structure of these sermons as they were presented may have been significantly different from these manuscripts.

The seven sermons were selected to help illustrate the instruction in the book. The sermons are drawn from a variety of biblical literature and provide creative perspectives on familiar stories. The sermon in Appendix 1 by Steve Mathewson and the sermon in Appendix 2 by Kent Edwards are expositions of Old Testament narratives. Mathewson relates his sermon from the vantage point of an imaginary character while Edwards chooses the perspective of a minor character mentioned in the narrative. In Appendix 3 Sid Buzzel demonstrates the exposition of a proverb. The main objective of most sermons from Proverbs is not so much explanation as application. This sermon seeks to illustrate and apply the main idea of the proverb. In Appendix 4, Haddon Robinson presents the Christmas story from Matthew's Gospel through a two-person dialogue with King Herod the Great. Appendices 5 and 6 each provide a woman's first-person perspective. Alice Mathews retells a well-known parable of Jesus from a fresh point of view in Appendix 5. The sermon in Appendix 6 is drawn from John's Gospel. Appendix 7, from Paul's letter to the Galatians, provides an example of a first-person exposition from a New Testament epistle. Both sermons in Appendices 6 and 7 focus on the resurrection of Jesus.

Appendix 8 is a bibliography of resources for the first-person preacher. The sources cited relate specifically to different aspects of the preparation and presentation of first-person sermons.

Thanks to Steve Mathewson, Kent Edwards, Sid Buzzel, and Alice Mathews for contributing their sermons. Each is truly exemplary.

Appendix 1

The following is a sermon by Steve Mathewson. Steve pastors Dry Creek Bible Church in Belgrade, Montana. The text that follows is the manuscript of a sermon originally preached in his church on Mother's Day, 1999.

Sermon Idea: God makes a difference in mothers who practice faithfulness to God and his people.

Subject: How does God make a difference in ordinary people?

Complement: He does it when they practice faithfulness to God and others.

Purpose: To enable ordinary people, especially mothers, to see how God can make a difference in them and through them.

Stance: During the days of the judges one of the elders from the town of Bethlehem steps forward in time to speak to the congregation at Dry Creek Bible Church on Mother's Day, 1999.

An Ordinary Hero

The Book of Ruth

If you're a mom, today is your big day. This is the one day of the year when your family pulls out all the stops and treats you like a queen. Dinner, flowers, maybe a gift or two. The kids even put on their best behavior. But just like the story of Cinderella, when this evening is over and the clock strikes midnight, you'll go back to your ordinary existence and all the ordinary stuff of being a mother. Let's face it. Being a mom means living a rather ordinary life. Most of you moms probably won't show up on the cover of *Family Circle,* nor will you have your own talk show or write your own book. It's not likely that Dr. Dobson will interview you on *Focus on the Family*. In other words, you're no different than the rest of us. Let's admit it. We're an auditorium full of rather ordinary people. Our biographies will probably never be published. We'll probably lack name recognition outside of our communities.

Unfortunately, we frequently confuse being ordinary with being insignificant. We're not convinced that ordinary people can make a real impact. We assume God uses those with incredible speaking ability, those with 30+ scores on their ACTs, those in powerful government posts. I turn to the Bible and read about kings, queens, or warriors whom God has used. Great, but I'm not sure I'm cut out of the same bolt of cloth. I'm ordinary. Wouldn't it be great to hear a story of an ordinary person whom God used to make a difference? Guess what! There is a book in the Bible that tells the story of an ordinary lady who became an ordinary mother. It's the story of Ruth. How did God make a difference through an ordinary person like Ruth? How does God make a difference through ordinary people like you and me?

This morning, I'd like to tell you the story of Ruth through the eyes of one of the eyewitnesses—one of the elders of Bethlehem, the little community where the events took place. How did this man see God using an ordinary person like Ruth? Please turn in your Bibles to the Book of Ruth. It starts on page 187 in the blue-covered Bible in front of you. You can check out the details as the story unfolds. If we could invite one of the elders of Bethlehem to tell us the story, it would sound something like this:

[*Bow head briefly, then walk to a different place on the platform and begin*]

By the world's standards, she wasn't much. She was ordinary, a lot like the ordinary people in our humble town. I ought to know . . . I spent my life there. Bethlehem . . . just another little town flanking a limestone ridge. For years, I served there as an elder on the town council.

Now there was a lady in our town who was ordinary, but God used her life to make a difference. Let me tell you what happened. It was the time when the judges were judging. I don't know if that means anything to you or not, but it was one of the darkest periods in our history. Our moral thermometer registered at an all-time low, and life stunk. I'm serious. Rape, violence, hunger, unemployment, hate crimes, inflation. You can read about it in the Bible in the Book of Judges.

The story begins during one of those recurrent famines. It happened the same way every time. Our nation would defy God's instruction, so God would send a guerrilla band to shake us up, and we'd end up in an economic mess, and, more often than not, a famine. It was during one of those famines when a mainstay in our community decided to pull up stakes. He decided to head to a neighboring nation with a better economy. Now that's fine for you if you need to relocate to make a better living. But for an Israelite to move . . . well, it amounted to saying, "in your face" to God. We were bound to the land for better or for worse. Ironically, this man's name was Elimelech. Do you have any idea what that means in our Hebrew language? It means, "my God is King." Well, "my God is King" up and turned his back on God and headed east to Moab. What a travesty! In your culture, you tell North Dakota jokes. We told Moab jokes. But it was more serious than that. To go to Moab was a shameful move. I'll explain in a moment.

Boy, were we upset! I remember pleading with Elimelech as he hitched up his team and loaded his cart: "Elimelech, you're making a big mistake. Don't go." But he wouldn't listen, stubborn old man. I got angry and called him a few nonkosher words . . . I won't even repeat them in Hebrew.

Now Elimelech had a family. He had a wife named Naomi. In our language that's the word "pleasant." Anyway, Naomi was caring for two frail boys: Mahlon and Chilion. Their condition was probably due to the famine. It was right during Naomi's pregnancy, and she simply didn't get enough to eat.

But things didn't go well in Moab either. The Elimelechs STRUCK OUT! For starters, Elimelech died on foreign soil. Strike one. Then the sons married Moabite girls. As God's people, we were forbidden to marry spouses from pagan nations. Strike two. And finally, the sons died. Strike three, and Naomi was out! Her husband was gone. Her sons were gone. And she was left with two widowed daughters-in-law—Moabites at that—and she was living in a foreign country.

Now about this time, Naomi began hearing rumors that the God of Israel was blessing the land of Israel and providing food. Since she struck out in Moab, it seemed like a good time to return. But what about her two daughters-in-law? Naomi wanted what was best for them, so she said: "Go back to your home. You've been good to me and to my sons. May God show you the *HESED* you showed to me and to my sons." *HESED* . . . I love that word. *HESED* means "loyal love" or "covenant love." Naomi continued, ". . . I could end up as a street person, and I don't want you to go through that. There are no other male sons to become your husbands. Even if I still had a husband—which I don't—by the time I gave birth and the boys grew old enough to marry . . . well, you couldn't wait that long. You're better off with your own families."

After shedding some tears and kissing good-bye, one of the gals, Orpah (not Oprah), took off for her home. But a funny thing happened. The other daughter-in-law, Ruth, whose name means "friendship," wouldn't budge! Her reply has become famous: "Where you go, I will go. Where you lodge, I will lodge. Your people, my people. Your God, my God. And where you die, I will die. That's where I will be buried."

[*Pause and move to another place on stage*]

It was late one afternoon, just about this time of year—early in May—when I was hauling a sack of barley into Bethlehem, that I noticed a group of people buzzing about the city gate. When I got closer, I could see a familiar, yet tired-looking face. And by her stood a pretty young lady who had a shy, but determincd look. My eyes swept back to the familiar face . . . and I figured out who she was just about the time one of the women said, "Is this really Naomi? It's Naomi, it's Naomi!" That's about the most exciting thing that had happened in our little town! But Naomi responded, "Don't call me Naomi." Remember Naomi is our word for "pleasant." She said, "Call me bitter, not pleasant, because Shaddai—the Almighty—has dealt with me bitterly. I went out full, but God has brought me back empty."

Naomi and Ruth were in dire straits. They had no food, no money, no Social Security checks. So Ruth decided to take matters into her own hands. In our culture, poor people were allowed to pick grain along the edges of a field, once the harvesters had gone through. And since the barley harvest was in full swing, Ruth requested her mother-in-law to let her go and do some gleaning.

Now I need to introduce somebody else—a man named Boaz. In our language, his name means "swift strength." In economic terms, he was our local Ted Turner. He had big bucks and big landholdings. Boaz also had a big heart. And here's the kicker . . . he was a relative of Elimelech—Naomi's deceased husband.

As Ruth headed outside of town to start gleaning, in whose field do you suppose she landed? Out of all the fields outside of town, in whose field did she end up? You guessed it . . . in the field of Boaz! I like the way our Hebrew Bible puts it: "Her chance chanced upon the field of Boaz." When Boaz came out later in the morning, he noticed her hard at work, and he inquired about her. He asked his crew chief, "Whose young woman is this?" That night, the crew chief told Boaz her whole life story and every move she had made that day! Boaz was touched. He was so moved that he told Ruth she didn't have to move on once she harvested the edge of the field. She could work right alongside the young ladies who were harvesting . . . in the field. And when she got thirsty, she could help herself to the water cooler.

Now Ruth was moved by all of this. She wanted to know why she had found Boaz's favor, especially when she was a foreigner—a Moabite! I told you earlier that Israelites despised Moabites. You see, God had told us not to let Moabites into our worship—even later-generation Moabites—because they had lured our people into sexual immorality years before when our people were poised to enter the Promised Land. So why had Ruth found favor from Boaz?

Boaz offered a moving reply: "I've been told all about what you have done for your mother-in-law since the death of your husband—how you left your father and mother and your homeland and came to live with a people you did not know before. May the LORD repay you for what you have done. May you be richly rewarded by the LORD, the God of Israel, under whose wings you have come to take refuge."

To Boaz and to us townspeople, Ruth's actions were incredible! Remember, this was the time when the judges were judging. We were living life in the fast lane, partying, doing whatever felt good, turning our backs on God. The one person who put her life in God's hands, who trusted his provision and his protection, was a Moabite! Of all people, Ruth was living responsibly while the rest of us were living irresponsibly!

Well, it was almost funny to watch Boaz. He sent Ruth a lunch invitation. Then, to top it off, he told his harvesters to be very discreet and nonchalant and drop some grain so that she could pick it up. "And most of all," he said, "do not give her a hard time." No Moabite jokes! When she finished the day, she had over half a bushel—a phenomenal amount for one day's work! And food enough for several days!

I wish I could have seen Naomi's response that night. I wasn't there, but I sure heard about it later. "The name of the man (yes) with whom I worked today (yes) is Boaz." YES!! Naomi was so excited that she used the "h" word . . . *HESED*. She said: "Blessed be Yahweh who has not abandoned his *HESED* (covenant love) to the living and the dead." Ruth had shown *HESED* to Naomi and her family. Now Yahweh was showing *HESED* to Naomi and her family.

Now why was Naomi so excited? Let me stop and explain something. If you were poor and had to lease your land to make ends meet like Elimelech had done, then a close relative—called a kinsman-redeemer—could buy out the lease and "release" it to you. Then, he could even lease it from you to provide you with an income. Either way, this person had to be a close relative who had the bucks and the willingness to do it. And you think your real estate laws are complicated! But Naomi had an even deeper problem than that. In our culture, childless widows were in a precarious situation. The family property and inheritance was passed down through the males. That's why, if you were a woman whose husband died and you had no male heir, your deceased husband's brother (are you following this?) would be responsible to take you as a wife and father a child for you. If he couldn't take the responsibility, it was passed down to other brothers and eventually to other close male relatives. Remember, you had to have a male heir.

Now maybe you can appreciate why Naomi got so excited when Ruth told her that she had worked all day in the field of Boaz. The wheels were turning in Naomi's mind. Boaz happened to be a close relative. That meant he could be a kinsman-redeemer—a relative who could step in and provide access to Naomi's husband's property and perhaps some income from it. Maybe, just maybe he could even be the relative who would marry Ruth and continue the family line. Boaz and Ruth . . . could it be a match made in heaven?

Anyway, Ruth worked in Boaz's field for the rest of the barley harvest and the wheat harvest. They had food. They had a safe place for Ruth to work—sad to say, there were some rather perverted people running around, even in Bethlehem. And maybe, just maybe there was a long-term solution to Naomi and Ruth's needs.

Well, the plot thickens. After the harvest was over, Naomi decided that it was time to make their move! She said to Ruth, "My daughter, should I not try to find a home for you, where you will be well provided for? Is not Boaz, with whose servant girls you have been, a kinsman of ours? Tonight he will be winnowing barley on the threshing floor."

Naomi wanted Ruth to try and get Boaz to fulfill both responsibilities—to be the husband who fathers an heir, and to be the close relative who bails them out of financial trouble. Here was her daring plan: Ruth would go down to the community threshing floor where Boaz was threshing his grain and make a proposal. That night, Boaz woke up with a sudden start. There was a woman lying at his feet . . . Ruth! He soon got over his grogginess when he realized what she wanted. The words may sound a little funny to you. Ruth asked, "Spread your covering over your maid, for you are a close relative." But what she was asking was this: "Take care of me and marry me." Imagine that, a woman asking a man to marry her!

Boaz, of course, was elated! And once again, that lovely word *HESED* popped up. "Ruth, this act of *HESED* is better than your first act towards your family. You could have gone after one of the young hunks wearing Wranglers. They've been dying to court you. Your life would be set. But then there would be no heir for Naomi. Ruth, the answer is yes. I will marry you. You are truly a woman of excellence."

"But," Boaz explained, "there's just one little hitch." You see, there happened to be a closer relative who had first dibs on Ruth. But Boaz had a plan. Funny that Boaz had this all figured out. So he sent Ruth home and told her to keep everything under wraps until he could take care of the closer relative.

I was at the gate the next morning. That's where we, the elders of the city, conducted our business. I think we were trying to hash out a settlement for a farmer who had two acres of grain trampled by his neighbor's oxen. Come to think of it, Boaz seemed kind of distracted. He was paying more attention to the people who entered through the city gate than he was to our little problem. Suddenly, he stood up and said, "Hey, buddy, come over here and sit down." With us elders as witnesses, Boaz explained the situation. At first, the man seemed willing to redeem Naomi's property. But when Boaz explained that he would have to take Ruth the Moabitess as his wife, well, he balked at that. And before it was done, this man passed on his option. He made his agreement official by giving his sandal to Boaz. This may seem like a crude way of filing an affidavit, but it did the job.

Well, I guess it was a match made in heaven! Naomi had some money to live on, Ruth had a husband, and both women would soon have a legitimate claim to the land and inheritance of their deceased husbands because Ruth gave birth to a son. They called his name Obed, or "servant." Ruth's boy, Obed, eventually had a boy of his own . . . Jesse. And one of Jesse's boys became a mighty king in Israel . . . David!

All of this came about because a rather ordinary woman, Ruth, practiced *HESED*—loving commitment. That's hard to do when everybody else is looking out for themselves. But God honors it. Yes, that's how he works: *God accomplishes great things through ordinary people who practice faithfulness to God and family.* It doesn't take "superman" or "supermom" to do that. You don't have to live life on the edge to make an impact. The only edge some of you know about is being on the edge when your four-year-old asks you her 437th question of the day, or your teen comes in twenty minutes late after his curfew. But even if you don't live on the edge, even if you're just ordinary, don't rule yourself out. God sees your day-to-day faithfulness to keep your children fed and clothed. He hears your prayers for them, and he hears your loving words of encouragement and sometimes rebuke when they head in the wrong direction. He sees you take a meal to a neighbor who is sick. He notices your efforts to make your community and your home a better place to live. The people of God who make the greatest impact do it through ordinary faithfulness . . . even when everybody else is faithless. The truth is, ordinary people who practice *HESED*—loving commitment—are not ordinary in God's sight.

Why, who knows what God might do through your faithfulness!

Appendix 2

The following is an edited transcript of a sermon by Kent Edwards. Edwards is the Director of the Doctor of Ministries program and a professor at Gordon-Conwell Seminary in South Hamilton, Massachusetts. The sermon was originally preached in chapel at Gordon-Conwell on November 28, 2000.

Sermon Idea: It takes faith and courage to be a leader of God's people.

Subject: What does it take to be a leader of God's people?

Complement: It takes courage that comes from a vital faith in God.

Purpose: For potential leaders to recognize how courageous they can be when they trust themselves to God.

Stance: Eliab travels forward in time to speak to the students at Gordon-Conwell Seminary.

The Profile of a Leader

1 Samuel 16–17

[*Introduction—Edwards begins as himself*]

Leaders influence our lives significantly. We know that in human history, leaders are often the hinge-points. Leaders can determine destiny. When you think of political leaders and the importance they play, you think of Napoleon, Alexander the Great, and Winston Churchill. We need leaders—strong leaders—in politics.

Leaders are important in the realm of sports. Two minutes left on the clock and Michael Jordan steps out on the court. You know there's going to be a difference. You know the difference leaders can make.

That's true in the church. You've been in churches where leaders have made a difference. They are men and women who dared to lead and make a difference in people's lives. We value leaders. And we should care about leaders.

I'd like to examine what it means to be a truly biblical leader. What it means to be a leader among God's people. You might want to follow me in your Bible—the Book of 1 Samuel, chapters 16 and 17—as we take a look at the life of one of the great leaders featured in Scripture.

This morning, I'd like to have this leader presented to you from the vantage point of someone who knew him well. He is part of the story. In the pages of Scripture, one of the dominant ways that God communicated truth is by telling us stories. So I'd like to take a lead from God's storybook and tell you a story from 1 Samuel 16–17. Follow along, if you would like. Or just sit back and listen. As you listen, you will discover what it means to be a leader.

[*Pause—Edwards assumes the first-person character*]

My name is Eliab. And you don't have a clue who that is, do you? All these years, I wondered if I would be famous, if I would be able to have my name etched into the history books of my country, into the hearts of its people. All these years, I've wondered if, when Eliab's name was spoken, people would gasp in awe and respect. And most of you haven't even heard of me.

I had my chance. I had my chance to be a leader. I lived in a time of transition, a time when there was a transfer of authority and power. Saul had been the king. And frankly, when he began, he did a good job. Saul had rallied the people together and rescued our countrymen, our affiliates in Jabesh-Gilead. He won a victory there that reverberated through the country. Confidence was high. Saul was the man. He was the leader.

And frankly, we all thought he should be the leader. He just looked like a leader. He had a thick head of hair. He had the stature and muscles that you just thought should belong to a leader. And he was head and shoulders above everyone else. He was tall. It's a good thing to be tall. He just looked like a leader.

But Saul got into trouble. Time and again, things went wrong for Saul. One time he went toe to toe with Samuel, the prophet. Samuel had spoken the word of the Lord to Saul. Samuel had given him instructions and told him what to do. But Saul had thought better of that. Saul had decided to do his own thing and to disobey God's word. Saul had taken liberties with God's word. And as Samuel came to him and confronted him, Saul refused to back down. Again and again, Samuel gave Saul the opportunity to repent, but Saul refused. He stood back and stood firm and stayed resistant. Finally, Samuel, with great defiance, with the authority that comes from being the spokesperson of God, said, "Even as you have rejected the word of the LORD, the LORD has rejected you."

I lived in a time of transition. Things were changing. Word spread like wildfire. Saul was on his way out. And everyone wondered who would be next. I wondered.

I didn't think I had a chance. You know, living in a place like Bethlehem, as I did, a little backwater town where no one ever goes. I felt no one would notice me. No one of stature really comes from Bethlehem. But on one occasion, we heard that Samuel was on the move. Samuel took with him the horn of anointing. This horn contained oil by which the next king would be anointed. That meant that someone was going to be selected king, and whoever it was might come from Bethlehem.

The elders were terrified. They didn't want to get caught in a power struggle between Saul and Samuel. Samuel assured them that he had only come to give sacrifice, which was true; he had come to do that. But he'd come to do more.

He asked to see my father. And it was then that my hopes rose. After all, if he wanted to talk to my father and he wanted to see his seven sons, then who else could he be waiting to anoint than me? After all, I'm Eliab, the oldest and the tallest. I looked like a leader. I had to work on the hair a bit. But a little bit of oil, slicked back, it looked pretty good. And I got a good robe, one that kind of cut down in the front, so I could make the hairs show. I tried to do that muscle thing. It didn't look quite as impressive as when Saul did it, but I was working on it. Still, it was clear that God was going to have me be the next king. For one, the profile. I mean isn't this a profile that would look good on a coin? You've got to have the looks to be a leader. I've got the height. I've got the profile. The hair and the muscles, I'm working on, but we can make improvements on it. I've got what it takes.

Samuel came to our family and he asked my dad, "Have your sons come before me." And I was ready. With all of my preparation, I even practiced my walk. And I did it well. Samuel was there with his horn, and I stood up straight, because I wanted to emphasize my height. As I walked, my robes filled out behind me. I looked beautiful. The hair was moving. Samuel was impressed. You could tell. He went for the horn, ready to anoint. He was on his way. Suddenly, as if somebody whispered in his ear, he hesitated, stopped. I kind of paused in my walk to give him a chance to reconsider. After all, I was here, the next anointed king, but he waited.

I stepped aside. My next brother came. Man, if he chose him, if he anointed him, we had to have a talk, Samuel and I. I knew what this kid did late at night. I had stories to tell. He wasn't leadership material. I could fill him in on what he didn't know. And I think Samuel went to anoint him, but he held back.

And the next one came and the next one. Finally, all seven of us are standing to the side. Well, this was a bust. We all walk in front of him and he doesn't anoint any of us. It doesn't say much for Samuel, does it? I mean, after all, he's supposed to be the one who hears the word of the Lord and we all come before him and where's the word of the Lord? What's going on?

Then Samuel says, "Are these all your sons?"

"Ah, sure . . . I mean, all but David. He's just a ruddy little kid. He's out with the sheep, lookin' after them. He's a, he's a boy. You certainly don't want David."

But Samuel said, "No, bring him. We're not going to eat until he comes."

When David finally arrived, a change came over Samuel's face, a look of confidence. He took the oil. He poured it on his head.

At dinner, I asked him why. I mean, why David? I've got the looks. I've got the hair. I practiced the walk. I have what it takes. Why David?

"Because," Samuel replied, "God said, 'People look on the outside. But I look at the heart.'"

From that moment on, things changed for David. The Spirit of the Lord came upon him. All the circumstances in the nation changed to favor him. He got called to the palace. Someone remembered he played the harp. I played instruments too, you know. Nobody asked me to go play for the king. But David gets summoned. He was obviously being ushered into a place where he could take over as the leader. That anointing is finding fruit in his life.

For a while I wondered, what did Samuel mean? "God looks at the heart." What is it about the heart? What is so different about David's heart and my heart? What makes him unique? Why did I walk by and not get chosen and why did David get the anointing? What is so different about the heart? What did God see about David's heart that made him unique, that qualified him as a leader?

Then I remembered a number of years before when the Philistines appeared. The Philistines were not nice people. They had an unfair military advantage. They knew how to smelt iron. They made weapons, swords, and javelins that gave them superiority on the battlefield. Of course, they'd used their smelting of iron for our benefit, but only in terms of agricultural implements. They wanted us to be able to grow more food, so they could come steal it. But on the battlefield, they had us beat, every time. And even though they belonged on the seacoast, they kept coming in farther and farther, making encroaches into our land. They knew that we were a bunch of farmers, that we couldn't stop them.

Then one time they came to the valley of Succoth, deep into our territory. And Saul did what any king should do. Saul sent out word for all the fighting men of Israel to come and gather. And come they did. The Philistines were there and their hordes. They gathered on one side of the valley up on the hill. The Israelites, we gathered on the other side. And I went with two of my brothers. After all, I had the potential of being a leader. I was tall. I had the hair. And I went to fight this battle.

It wasn't a battle like others though. We were getting ready and they were getting ready. In the midst of our preparations, suddenly the Philistine hordes parted. Out came this, this giant. He was unlike anything any of us had ever seen before. He stood over nine feet tall. I wondered if he was part of the giants of days gone by, back when our people first came to the edge of the Promised Land and considered themselves grasshoppers compared to the people who lived there. I don't know. I felt like a grasshopper looking at this man. Nine feet tall! As he moved, the ground started to shake. He lumbered with authority and power. His arms were the size of tree trunks. He was massive! And he was a warrior trained in the arts from the earliest of his days. He was a powerful, formidable man, and not only physically, but also in how he was decked out.

A bronze helmet. A shirt of mail that weighed 150 pounds. Some of our soldiers didn't even weigh 150 pounds. His shirt weighed 150 pounds, all carefully constructed, so that nothing could get to him. If someone's sword struck Goliath, it would bounce off that shirt and he'd be safe. And in case anyone decided to ignore the upper-body and take his legs out, this giant had bronze greaves on his legs to protect him. He had a javelin strapped to his back. The Philistines were excellent with javelins. This was a huge instrument. The tip was made of iron and it alone weighed fifteen pounds. We wondered what strength you would need to throw something like that. He had a spear in his hand that was bigger yet.

As if that wasn't enough, he had a soldier to hold his shield. The shield was the size of a picnic table. It could be moved in front of him, so that he was always protected against the onslaught of the enemy. This man was enormous. And we were intimidated.

Goliath steps forward. He stands in front of his army and us, and he defies the armies of God. Goliath yells to us, "You servants of Saul. Why should we all fight? Just send one man, if you have one, to come and do battle with me. And if he beats me and kills me, we all will serve you. But if I defeat him and kill him, then you will all serve me. Come send a man, send a man."

Well, none of us really felt like going right then. We were busy. You know, we had things to do. Get ready for battle, all that kind of stuff.

Next morning came. Saul had to do something. So we got ready for battle. All the preparations were made. We got together and he gave us the pep talk. We were getting ready for the battle. And we all ended with the war cry, getting ready for the charge down the hill to meet the Philistines. We began our charge. He was big! RUAHH! RUAHH! We were ready! RUAHH! We started down the hill and Goliath walked up. Ruahh!? . . . oohah . . . "You know," we reasoned, "anyone thought of lunch? I'm ready to, you know, take a break." And we walked back.

It happened that morning. It happened that night. It happened the next day, and the day after and the day after. Ten days. Twenty days. Thirty days! Every day, twice a day, we were scared back by Goliath.

Time went on and Saul needed to do something. He decided that we needed some incentive. The troops needed more motivation to get out and fight. So he said, "What we need is a champion. Who's going to go forward? If you volunteer"—he wasn't going to volunteer, but if any of us volunteered—"I'll make you wealthy. I'll give you my daughter for a wife. And you'll never pay taxes."

It was interesting, after that announcement, what people talked about around the campfires. Kept talking about how money was really the root of all evil. How they were all happily married or they had a sweetheart back home. And frankly, they enjoyed paying taxes. It was their way of contributing to society, their way of helping out others. They would feel unimportant and neglected if they weren't allowed to pay their fair share. They didn't want to fight.

After forty days, I was embarrassed. We were all embarrassed. What made it worse though was my dad sent David, this ruddy little shepherd, to bring food. He brought some grain and some cheeses for our commanding officers. And he came all the way to the front lines. Frankly, I was embarrassed to have my brother stand there and see us go forward to do our Ruahh cry, only to retreat to safety again. I didn't want him to see that. He arrived after forty days to see the state of the battle and it hadn't even started. I was ashamed.

David came and he began to talk to the other soldiers. I tried to get rid of him. I wanted to intimidate him, to make him leave. I snapped, "Who are you? What are you doing here, you little kid? Why aren't you back home with the sheep looking after them? I know your heart. You're wicked. You're only here to gaze at the corpses. You're here for the wrong reason. Get out of here, kid!"

I could see the hurt in his face, but he didn't buckle. He didn't go home. He kept asking everyone about what was going on. What was the problem? He found out it was Goliath and his attitude was, "Just Goliath?"

It didn't take long for word about David to get back to Saul. Saul called him to his tent. We knew what they were talking about. You can't have a conversation in a tent and not have word get out. David told Saul, "I'll fight him."

Saul says, "You are going to fight Goliath? You're not a warrior. You're a baby. You're a child."

David replied, "I have fought a bear and I have fought a lion to protect my flock and God has been with me there. God can protect me against Goliath." The boy had confidence. The boy had faith.

Frankly, Saul was caught off guard. David had faith he didn't have, that none of us had. After forty days, no one else came forward, not Saul's son Jonathan, no one, only David.

Saul agreed. When you think about it, what did he have to lose? Forty days of nothing happening, something had to give. If this is the only one who would volunteer, then let him volunteer. Saul tried to put his own armor on David, but frankly it looked ridiculous. Saul's armor hung all over him. David pushed it aside. "I'm not used to it." That's a polite way of saying, "Get rid of all this stuff."

Then David prepared to battle Goliath. He went down to the brook and gathered five smooth stones. He put four of them in his shepherd's bag and one in his sling. You know what a sling is? A little pocket of leather, two straps, a foot and a half long, each side. He put the stone in the sling and walked towards Goliath.

Goliath had come for his daily rant when he saw David. He couldn't believe it: "Am I a dog that you send a boy to fight me with sticks? He doesn't have a weapon. He doesn't have anything. You're sending a boy against me?"

When the giant realized that David wasn't backing away, he began to get angry: "You come here, boy. You come here and I'll feed your carcass to the birds of the air and the beasts of the field. I'll serve you up for dinner."

I was never so proud of David right then at that moment and never so shocked. He looked Goliath in the eye and he said, "You come against me with sword and spear, but I come against you in the name of the Lord Almighty. And today, I will kill you and cut off your head and serve you to the beasts of the field and the Philistines to the birds of air. And everyone will know that a battle is not won by sword and spear, but by the name and the power of God."

Goliath was seething. You could almost feel his hatred, even at a distance. He roared a guttural animal roar and started to move towards David.

David stood at a distance. The Philistines used javelins and spears. They didn't use bows and arrows. So their range was limited. And David kept his distance. He stood far away where Goliath couldn't get him. But more than that, David used his other advantage. He was fast. That little brother of mine may be small and young, but he had wings on his feet. He could fly.

He started swinging his sling, swinging it around and around. He's flying. Goliath's shield bearer doesn't know what to do. He's trying to move the picnic table. David is racing around. Soon the picnic table is out of position. Goliath kind of lumbers. He may be big, but Goliath isn't fast. He tries to take a couple of steps towards David. David is flying. He's crouching low. I've seen that stance before. At that moment, he pushes off with his right foot, whirls the sling and then one of the strings lets go and the stone flies towards Goliath. You could almost hear it fly. The sound of hundreds of thousands of warriors holding their breath was deafening. Finally, that stone hit its mark.

Goliath fell to his knees . . . down on his face. It was over that fast. The shield bearer's standing there dumbstruck at everything that's going on around him. David comes up to Goliath, and pulls out Goliath's own sword. David didn't have a sword; only Saul and Jonathan had swords. David pulled out Goliath's own sword, cut off his head, and held it up in the air.

The fellow holding the shield decided that he wanted to be somewhere else. And he beetled up the hill, back towards the Philistines. The Philistine army also decided that backwards was a good direction. If this boy could kill their champion, what could all of the rest of the army do? They started running, running as fast as they could. Then the Israelites decided, if David could do this, they could do more. And for the first time in forty days, our Ruahh! meant RUAHH! Let's get them. And we chased them for miles and miles. Thousands of the Philistines were killed. We plundered their camp.

The fate of our nation changed because of one person, a ruddy little kid. His heart was different than mine. He had the heart of a leader. He had a heart of courage. He had a heart of faith. That's what made David the greatest leader of God's people. I didn't have a heart of faith. That's why you don't know my name.

When you know what God wants you to do, do it. Even if no one else believes God, you believe him. Be a leader. Have a heart of courage! Have a heart of faith!

Appendix 3

The following is an edited transcript of a sermon by Sid Buzzel. Buzzel is Professor of Bible Exposition at Colorado Christian University in Denver, Colorado. This sermon was originally preached at the Heritage Baptist Church in Aurora, Colorado, in the fall of 1990.

Sermon Idea: Guard your heart.

Subject: Why must you guard your heart?

Complement: Because all your life is centered there.

Purpose: For listeners to understand how important it is to guard their thinking and their feelings.

Stance: The preacher spins a modern-day parable to illustrate the truth of the ancient proverb.

The Story of Anna McLeash

Proverbs 4:23

I heard from Jacob Ivan Weaver, "Sonny" his friends called him. We were friends in college back in 1961. Sonny and I were working our way through school and so we had a special relationship with each other and with Mrs. Richards down in the employment office.

Sonny and I had grown up working hard. He grew up in a Mennonite home in western Pennsylvania—with a work ethic, an honest ethic. Our Mennonite brothers and sisters have given us an enviable track record as Christians of being people who are dependable. And Sonny was that kind of a person. With a name like Jacob Ivan Weaver, how could you be any other way?

Well, the job that was posted in our mailboxes was an unusual one and we were the two who were offered this particular job. I was tied up on the weekend that the job was available and so there was no question, as we went down and visited with Mrs. Richards, that Sonny was to drive out to Bryn Mawr, Pennsylvania, out where the great lavish estates were. And he was to meet Anna McLeash to do some work at her estate.

He was given an elaborate set of instructions. He was to drive out there. He was to arrive precisely at 9:30. He was to push the button outside of the great iron gate that closed off the entrance, the only entrance of a huge stone wall that went all the way around this vast estate out there in Bryn Mawr, Pennsylvania.

He arrived a few minutes early and sat in his car. At precisely 9:30 he pushed the button and a voice came out of the speaker that was there and said, "What is your name and what is your business?"

He said, "My name is . . ." He didn't know whether to use Jacob Ivan or Sonny. This was a rather ominous thing, so he said, "Mr. Weaver. And I'm from Philadelphia College of the Bible and I am to meet Anna McLeash to do some work."

She asked him a few other questions to make sure that he was, in fact, J. Ivan "Sonny" Weaver, the Mennonite boy from western Pennsylvania who had been sent by Mrs. Richards to do work for Anna McLeash.

When that was all cleared, these iron gates rolled back on their tracks and he drove his car through. And he went through some lovely trees and then across a wide open, beautifully manicured lawn, up to another iron fence that was around the house, with another set of gates in the iron fence, and another speaker, and another set of questions.

Finally, these gates too rolled back on their track and he drove up to the house and went up to the front porch as he was instructed, and a lady met him on the porch and asked him for some identification. He showed her his student card and his driver's license. She read them and was satisfied and invited him in the house.

There he sat with Anna and her elderly mother. They visited. They interrogated him at length, finding that he was truly a nice young man. They had called the Bible College thinking that of course at a Bible College you would get nice young men or women. People who were preparing for the clergy or some other such profession, and who had a good moral and spiritual background or they wouldn't be at a school like that.

And she gave him a list of jobs to do. They didn't seem all that terribly important that he would have to be such a trusted individual to do these kinds of jobs. But he spent the rest of the day doing jobs and she paid him about twice the going rate. And Sonny went back out through the two sets of iron gates and went home.

About a week and a half later there was another message. Anna McLeash wanted only Sonny Weaver. Nobody else was to apply. Same arrangement—specific time, specific questions, two iron gates. He didn't have to show her his identification this time, but he went into the house, he visited with Mom and Anna at length and was given another list of jobs to do.

A week later, a third call. Same instructions, same kind of visit. Then Anna said, "Sonny, I think now I can ask you to do the job that we really need to have done. We needed the other jobs done, and we're glad we found you, we always have jobs to be done here and we have to have somebody we can trust, but this job you had to be checked out for."

So she took him into a back part of the house that he had never been in before. He hardly knew that it was there. And on one wall of this room in the back of the house there seemed to be a hole. It didn't look like a door, it was just an opening in the wall. And she led him through that opening in the wall and they went down the carpeted stairs into a lovely family room, a den, downstairs. On one wall were books and she told Sonny to turn and look at the books and not to look back until she told him to.

So he stood and looked at the books. In a few seconds she said, "okay." And he turned around and there in the paneled wall was an opening and another room. And they entered that other room, down there in the basement, behind the paneled wall. And as he went in, he noticed a number of file cabinets and a lovely antique desk. But what caught his attention was one whole wall that was an enormous door to a vault. It looked like the vaults you see in a bank. It had a big wheel on the front.

What Anna needed was somebody to move all of the files and that desk from down in the ominous-looking room to a study on the second floor where she would work. And she explained that her father, Seamus McLeash, used to work in the vault before he died. He taught her how to take care of the family books and accounts, which were stored in these file cabinets. But she'd seen too many Bella Lagosi movies and she didn't like going down into the basement. Although it was lovely and lavishly done, it still had the feeling of Frankenstein coming out of the vault. She wanted it all moved upstairs, but there was obviously no way she could move those things herself, so she needed help. That's why Sonny was called out there.

Seamus McLeash had made millions in the copper smelting business, mining and smelting copper from South America. But that was the second fortune he had made in the copper business. In the twenties he had made another fortune. But during the bank crash and the stock market crash and the depression, he found himself penniless. And he lived those hard, hard days of deprivation. And during those difficult days, he made a decision. The decision was, I will be rich again, but nobody will ever take it away from me.

So he started off in business and as quickly as he could save up enough money, he bought gold and silver. He had places in the backyard where he would dig holes and bury his riches in iron boxes. And he had dogs in the backyard. They ran around in the backyard and made their own deposits. He didn't like that. But these dogs had a smile like the grill of a '48 Buick, and people would say, "We don't need to go in that backyard for any reason we can think of."

Finally he had enough saved up to buy this piece of property in Bryn Mawr, Pennsylvania, out on the main line, an enormous estate. He built this huge wall around it and he put broken glass, cemented broken glass, all around the top of that wall. And he put up an iron fence inside that wall and he put a fortress inside the iron fence and then he built this enormous vault in the basement with this big door and he said, "No bank is going to get my money. I will guard what I have worked for. I will guard this to protect my family, my daughter, and my wife, and my children's children, and my children's children's children."

And Seamus taught Anna well. He taught her about all of the security systems. He told her to keep her mouth shut. No one was to know. "Don't trust anyone with anything," he warned. "Guard what's yours and guard it carefully." So Sonny spent the day moving all of the records upstairs and the file cabinets and the desk and then he went home.

Sonny continued to get calls periodically to go out, visit with Anna, do whatever jobs she needed done. He was now trusted to go into parts of the house to paint or to do repairs where no worker was ever allowed to go.

One day, he went to the estate and when the door opened, Anna came bounding out on the porch. And Anna was different today. Her hair was fixed. She had makeup on. She had on a new dress, a designer type dress. Her voice was different. Her smile was different. Sonny said she did a little dance, sort of like a dance. It looked like a hippo that stepped in something nasty, but it was kind of a dance, the best Anna could do, given the circumstances.

And so there she was, and Sonny said, "Anna, you look . . . you look . . . different today."

And she said, "I feel different. Since the last time you were here, I met a man, a wonderful man, a charming man, a man with a great vocabulary. His name is Tom Post and I'm in love." Sonny was happy for her. She said, "In a few hours, Tom Post is coming out here and I can't wait for you to meet him."

Sure enough, about noon, Tom Post did pull up in his sports car. And he was debonair, suave, and handsome. He had a wonderful vocabulary, "a way with words," as Anna put it. But as they visited, Sonny began to get an uneasy feeling about Tom Post. What Anna described as debonair, Sonny saw as smooth. What she saw as suave, he defined as slimy. What she saw as a man with great words, he saw as a man with a line a mile long. We decided later that, rather than call him Tom Post, maybe compost fit him better.

But Anna was in love. And the next time Sonny went out, she gave him a large bonus and said, "I've appreciated knowing you. You're a wonderful young man, but we won't need you anymore. Tom feels that he can do these sorts of things, and it's better not to have too many people around." That was the end of the Anna McLeash story—for two years.

In the spring of 1963, Sonny got another call. Anna asked him to bring some other students with him to help her move. Sonny thought she must have gotten married. So a group of students and Sonny went out, and the great iron gate was open. They drove through, up to the great iron fence, and that gate was open. And he went up and for the first time ever he just knocked on the door. He had never had the chance to knock on the door before because of all the security. Anna was always on the porch to meet him.

She opened the door. Sonny said she was the most disheveled mess you ever saw in your life. Her hair was barely combed. She looked drawn and tired. Sonny said, "So you're moving!"

She said, "Yes, I'm moving."

He got his crew working and he said, "Anna, can we talk?"

And she said, "Yes, I guess so." They went into the kitchen and she sat down at the table and began to sob uncontrollably.

Sonny said, "Anna, what's wrong?"

She said, "I don't know where I'm going to go."

He said, "What happened?"

She said, "Well, Tom Post talked of marriage. Tom Post said that I should not only take care of my children, and my children's children, and my children's children's children, but for generation after generation we should take care. He told me of the Kennedys and the Rockefellers and the Vanderbilts and the people with legendary fortunes. And he said the way they have built these legendary fortunes, which will go on forever and ever, is to invest them wisely and properly. My father had been so against any type of investment, he had been blindly against any kind of investment, but Tom was very persuasive.

"He said the reason he wanted the generations of my children to be cared for is that he wanted my children's children's children, to be his children's children's children. Ahh, what music to my ears, that this gorgeous man would want me. He proposed marriage in a formal kind of way. I asked him if we would become engaged. And he said, 'Certainly, when the time was right.' He couldn't do it right then. He never really explained. I wouldn't have heard it anyway. I was so taken."

To make a complicated and long story short, what he did was convince Anna that she should allow him to invest her money. And then, since he was traveling so much, and a lot of these deals had to be made on the spot, that if she gave him power of attorney she would not have to be involved. He could just take care of it. She could have parties. She could travel. She wouldn't even have to worry about the money because he would take care of it for them. And he had a great interest in it now because he was going to marry her.

Well, this went on for two years and on one of his trips (he had been away for a month), she received a letter from an attorney. It was a corporate attorney. And the letter told her that the house in which she lived belonged to the corporation for which he worked and she as a rational person could certainly understand that this corporation could not have somebody living on their property. She had sixty days to move out.

She read the letter again. This couldn't be. How could this happen? Surely this was a mistake. She tried to call Tom at one of the numbers he had left her, but she could not locate him. So she called one of her father's attorneys. He came out immediately. He read the letter and said, "This is absurd. I'll check on it for you."

He took the letter and did some checking. He found that over the two years, Tom Post had laundered her entire fortune into his own accounts. It was covered up in such a way that it was impossible to get it back. The lawyer tried. His whole firm tried.

Sonny moved Anna. He heard from her a few more times and that was the end of the story. He never knew what happened to Anna McLeash until a couple of weeks ago. He read an article in the *Philadelphia Inquirer*. The article stated that Anna

McLeash, the daughter of the wealthy and deceased Seamus McLeash, was found dead in the 1700 block of Arch Street, a homeless indigent.

If Anna McLeash had known what I am about to tell you, she would not have lost her fortune. She would not have lost her dignity. She would not have lost her purity that she had so jealously guarded for her husband someday. She would not have lost everything that her father had left her and taught her to carefully guard. She wouldn't have lost all that. Because the words I'm about to tell you are not my words. They are not words that I have thought up to protect you from losing the most valuable things, things which oftentimes can never be reclaimed. They are words from God. They are words that are given us from God through Solomon, the wisest man who ever lived. They are very simple words: "Above all else, guard your heart, for it is the wellspring of life."

"Above all else, guard your heart, for it is the wellspring of life" (Prov. 4:23). You should memorize it. You should have your children memorize it. You should teach them what it means. You should teach them how to guard their hearts. You see, what no robber or burglar had ever been able to do by use of force, Tom Post had done. He had scaled the wall. He walked through the fence. He found the weak point. It was not the iron gate. It was not the iron fence. It was not the security system. It was not the hidden room in the basement. It was not the door to the vault. None of those were weak links.

For all the educating and all of the preparing for life that Seamus and Jenine McLeash had so carefully prepared for Anna, they had failed to tell her, "Anna, guard your heart." Guard your money. Guard your purity. Guard your intellect. Guard your body. But above all else, they should have told her, guard your heart.

The story I have told you is true, just as a parable is true. Anna and Tom Post didn't really exist, but they do. They are like thousands of people who try to be secure, but they have not secured their hearts. Don't give your heart to anyone or anything that is not absolutely trustworthy. Start by giving your heart completely to God. All the issues of life are settled when you do that.

Appendix 4

The following is a sermon manuscript by Haddon Robinson. Robinson is Distinguished Professor of Preaching at Gordon-Conwell Theological Seminary in South Hamilton, Massachusetts. The sermon was originally presented by Robinson as a dialogue with Torrey Robinson, pastor at the First Baptist Church in Tarrytown, New York, on December 23, 2001.

Sermon Idea: Worship Jesus as Lord or reject him, but don't ignore him.

Subject: How can we respond to the Lordship of Jesus Christ?

Complement: We either reject him because he threatens us or we worship him.

Purpose: To have people understand the crucial issues involved in Christmas.

Stance: King Herod the Great is released from his torment in hell to tell his story to the pastor and congregation at the First Baptist Church in Tarrytown.

Setting the Record Straight

Matthew 2:1–18

This morning I would like to introduce you to a man that historians refer to as "Herod the Great." He played an important role at the birth of Jesus, and I thought it would be proper to have him here since we are about to celebrate Christmas. Welcome, King Herod.

I appreciate the opportunity to be here. I haven't had a chance to defend myself for centuries. I have been insulted and demeaned and I am determined to set the record straight.

You're going to have to pardon me, but how do I address you? Are you comfortable with the title "Herod the Great"?

Of course I'm comfortable with it! Historians granted me that title. It sets me apart from those lesser Herods like my son and grandsons. I alone am Herod the Great, and I worked hard to earn that title.

Then you wanted to be famous?

Doesn't everybody? That's part of the punishment where I come from. We get exactly what we have always wanted. I determined to be the greatest ruler of my time. And I was. I earned the title "Herod the Great." People like you want to demean me. You don't appreciate who I am and what I accomplished.

I didn't mean to offend you. It's just that the title "Herod the Great" strikes me as being, well . . .

Too strong? Well, I am somebody. Every time someone like you reads what that tax collector Matthew wrote about me, I am demeaned. Every time some child dressed in a bathrobe with a paper crown stuck on his head plays me in one of your obnoxious Christmas pageants, I am demeaned. In one of your churches, one of those urchins announced to everyone that he was Harold the Grape. What's that make me? An old prune? No, I tell you, I am Herod the Great!

Well then, let's get to it. I understand, King Herod, that you were a cruel tyrant. In fact, Matthew said you wanted to murder Jesus when you heard about him.

Listen, you have to do what you have to do. I had to rule with a firm hand. Being a leader isn't easy, you know. You can't take power for granted. That was particularly true in my situation.

Oh? What exactly was your situation?

I was a politician. I was no amateur at politics, either. I grew up in a political family. Caesar himself made my father a Roman citizen and exempted him from paying any taxes for his entire life. In fact, my father served for a while as procurator of Judea, and then he got Cassius, the emperor, to appoint me as governor of Galilee in what you call 47 B.C.

So you started your political career as a young man?

I was twenty-five years old. I made the most of that position when I got it. Even the Jews I ruled over admitted that I was a good administrator. I used the military to keep order in the region. It wasn't easy. I had to govern my area well. I also had to kiss up to the political machine in Rome. It was like walking on a narrow road with steep ditches on either side. It was difficult and dangerous.

I don't understand what you mean. What made it so difficult?

Let me give you an example. Five years after I took office (42 B.C.), Cassius who appointed me to my position was defeated by Mark Antony. I had to scramble. I made a trip to Rome and I convinced Mark Antony and the Roman senate that I could be trusted. They not only reappointed me to my position in Galilee, but they also made me king of Judea. When they gave me that title it was empty. The Parthians had taken over Judea and Jerusalem. If I was going to be king, I had to bring the region back to an allegiance to Rome. I used my army and moved south and took control of the region. It took three years to do it, but I did it. That made me king in deed as well as title.

That title, "King of the Jews," must have been very satisfying to you. After all, you got what you wanted.

It wasn't what you might think. I couldn't relax. You see I was only half Jewish. My father was an Idumaean. The Romans didn't completely trust me because I was a Jew and the Jews didn't respect me because they felt I was a half-breed. Standing in the middle isn't easy ground to occupy. You get hit on every side. Let's be honest. Judea as a region was nothing to the Romans. They considered it a little backwater property that gave them nothing but trouble and I could never be completely sure of their support.

How did you handle your new position?

I had no illusions that I could get the Jews to love me or even respect me. But I determined to make them fear me. If they wouldn't willingly give me their support, then I had to rule them by force. It was the only thing for me to do. They wouldn't admit this, but I did it for them.

For them? You mean the Jews?

Yes, of course, the Jews. If I hadn't kept them in line, the Romans would have sent in their armies and smashed them like roaches. That would have been far worse for everyone, wouldn't it? Wouldn't it?

I suppose so. But you have a reputation for going far beyond what you needed to do to keep order.

What do you know about keeping order? You have to exert your will unless you want to end up as somebody's rug. You can't let enemies walk all over you. If you want to succeed in the power game, you have to get them before they get you!

But you were savage. You were brutal . . .

That depends on how you look at it. From your perspective it might look brutal, but believe me it was necessary.

But didn't you have your wife Mariamne and your sons murdered?

I had no choice. You've got to understand. You have to do what you have to do. I didn't marry Mariamne for romance. The marriage was political. The woman was a Hasmonaean. The Hasmonaeans were my chief rivals. So I married her to try to turn my enemies into friends. It didn't work out the way I planned. You know, once a Hasmonaean, always a Hasmonaean. She and her sons plotted against me.

Were you sure of that? Completely sure?

I had my suspicions. So I got rid of them. If you're serious about power, you've got to protect it or you'll lose it. You have to do what you have to do. Besides I had nine other wives and other sons. I didn't really need them.

But you have to admit that it takes a pretty brutal man to wipe out members of his own family.

You still don't get it, do you? Look, all of us use power to get what we want. I suppose you think none of you would ever do that. Have you ever felt threatened? Have you been jealous? Have you ever wanted to get rid of somebody? To cut that individual out of your life? Oh, you wouldn't consider murder. You don't have the stomach for it. But you'll do it in other ways.

In other ways? What do you mean?

You'll savage people with your tongue. You'll tear them down. You cut people out of your life. All kinds of people want to be free of their wives and husbands. They go through a court to get their dirty work done. Don't look down your nose at me. We do what we have to do to protect ourselves and get our way. I am no different than any of you.

Well, what about the events recorded by Matthew about you? You wanted to murder infants.

You had to bring that up, didn't you? You ignore all the things I did that made me great. Why don't you ask me about my buildings? I was a great builder. During the forty-one years of my reign I built theaters, amphitheaters, hippodromes. I introduced athletic games in honor of Caesar. I constructed cities and rebuilt fortresses. All of them were important, lasting public works projects. I built palaces throughout the country. I built Jewish temples in Gentile territory. Have you been to Israel?

Yes. I have.

Then you must have seen the magnificent ruins of what I built. I started the rebuilding of the Jewish temple in Jerusalem. It took eighty-eight years to complete, but I started it. I used massive stones to construct it. The dome of that temple was covered with gold. Pilgrims climbing up to the temple had to shield their eyes because the dome was as brilliant as the sun. Do you know what one rabbi said of that temple? He said, "If you have not seen the temple in Jerusalem, then you have never seen a beautiful building." They call that structure Herod's Temple. That's what made me great. But you don't think about that at all, do you? That tax collector Matthew never mentions it. All you want to talk about are those astrologers and that baby.

Well, tell us about them. Do you remember them?

Of course I do. In light of the way things turned out, how could I forget? One afternoon I was in my chambers talking with one of my builders when one of my aides came to tell me that we had visitors . . . Gentiles . . . who had come from a distance. He said that they seemed to have some importance. They were asking questions around the city of Jerusalem and he thought I should meet them. I was tempted to put them off. What could Gentiles like them do for someone like me? But because of the way my aide talked, I worked them into my schedule.

What did you think of them?

Well, they entered my rooms and after the usual formalities, they got right down to business. They asked me what they were asking everyone else: "Where is he who has been born King of the Jews? We have seen his star in the East, and we have come to worship him."

Why did they ask you that question?

I've wondered that myself. I suppose they came to Jerusalem because it was the capital city. But I had heard nothing about a king. Certainly, I had had no new children.

What did you tell them?

Oh, let's stop all of this. You know what I did. You've heard the story so many times; you're bored with it. You sing songs about the "wise men," as you call them. They were stupid. If you have an ounce of good sense, you don't approach a sitting king and ask about a new king that has been born.

So you were bothered by their question?

This talk about a new king represented a threat to me and my power. The Jews were longing for a messiah, a deliverer who would save them from the Romans and take them out of their troubles. For centuries they were expecting this savior. My advisors and I didn't take this talk about a baby born to be a king that seriously. But messiahs can create themselves. Mix desperate longings with fanatic religion and you can produce a messiah.

So you were worried?

Concerned. Frankly, I didn't know what to make of those astrologers from the East. But I couldn't ignore what they said. I had to get to the bottom of it. So I assembled a committee of theologians and scholars and asked what they knew about this messiah. They said that according to their Scriptures there was a messiah who was to come from Bethlehem—that's a small village about five miles south of Jerusalem. My advisors didn't put much stock in what these visitors said, though. Not one of them was interested enough to take a quick trip down to Bethlehem to see if anything was going on. But you can't be too careful if your power is being threatened. So I gave those astrologers directions to Bethlehem, and I told them to report back to me.

Did you think that they would come back and tell you if they had found the baby they were looking for?

Why not? I went along with their questions. I told them that I desired to worship the child along with them. But they betrayed me. I waited a couple of weeks and when they didn't come back through the city, I was worried. I wondered if they had found something, or someone.

But, Your Highness, Matthew says that you had little boys around Bethlehem slaughtered. You were heartless. You murdered your wife, your three sons, your mother-in-law, your uncle, and hundreds of others during your reign, but these were toddlers and infants.

Stop it. I did what anyone in power would do. Kings, dictators, presidents, we all do it. One way or another you protect yourself. You have to do what you have to do.

But helpless infants couldn't possibly have hurt you. You were heartless.

Perhaps it sounds that way to you. The whole thing was blown out of proportion just to slander me. And it hasn't helped to have the church refer to the incident as the Slaughter of the Innocents. Slaughter of the Innocents makes it sound like hundreds or even thousands. How many boy babies do you think were in a town like Bethlehem? There weren't five hundred men in the whole community. At the most, there were thirty or forty boys. Just toddlers. No value to anyone.

But small children are precious.

Are they? Are they really? In your culture you kill over a million of them a year before they are born. You see them wiped out in the streets of your cities or in Belfast or Bosnia or Africa where they starve to death. You go on eating your supper.

But if Jesus born in Bethlehem was God's messiah, and your theologians said that he might be, why would you risk setting yourself up against God?

I was threatened, I tell you. You do all kinds of things when you are afraid. I was threatened. Fear makes you strike out, doesn't it? Have you ever felt threatened by someone?

Oh, sure, but . . .

Then you know how it feels. Listen to me. You ought to feel threatened now. Threatened by that baby. After all, he didn't stay a baby, some cuddly infant you can carry around. That's what I want to say to you. You should feel threatened. I have known about him for two thousand years. It does me no good now. I should have wiped him out when I had the chance. But it wouldn't have stopped him. My son, Herod Antipas, conspired with a Roman named Pilate to put him to death. They succeeded. The two of them had him crucified. They killed him. But they couldn't get rid of him. He actually came back from the dead. How do you deal with someone like that? He's a king as I could never have been a king. He's eternal. He threatens any kingdom builder, I tell you. That's why he's dangerous.

But, Your Highness, I don't understand. What do you mean by dangerous?

He threatens all of us. All the things we trust in and cherish. He's no sweet little lamb. He's more like a lion. People are deceived by him. They don't recognize his power.

I don't think many men and women in our day feel threatened by him.

They should. Don't you Christians refer to him as "Lord"?

Yes, we refer to him as "the Lord Jesus Christ."

Do you know what you are saying? Do you? You have areas of life in which you want to be Lord. Everybody does. You build your little kingdoms with walls you design to keep him out. Your business, your bank accounts, your sex life, your relationships. You keep those little territories away from him. But I'll tell you this: you and that baby can't both be Lords.

And you, King Herod, your throne, your title, your buildings, were they most dear to you?

Of course they were. I gave my life to rule and to build. Then I died and left all that I built behind. But he remained. That baby is no lamb. He is a lion disguised as a lamb.

Yet the Bible presents him both ways, a lion and a lamb.

I came to warn you. Christmas isn't for children. You engage in that sentimental drivel about winter and toy soldiers and chestnuts roasting on some fire. You have those pageants staged by unsuspecting children, featuring Herod the Great. Laugh if you want to. But Christmas isn't what you make it out to be. Christmas threatens everything you hold with a tight fist.

What exactly should we do with Christmas?

Think about it, man; think about it. Christmas means that a new king has been born, an eternal king. You can do one of two things with him. You can fall down and worship him as Lord and surrender your life and all of your little kingdoms, dreams, and designs to him. Or you can quit your game playing and get rid of him. Get as far away from him as possible.

So, King Herod, that's what you want to tell us? That's what you really want to tell us?

I had my opportunity. I had my chance. I made my choice against him. Now I'm linked to that reality for eternity. Everyone who has heard about the baby king born in Bethlehem makes a choice. Will he be a king that you worship, or a king that you ignore or defy? I tell you this. He will either save you or judge you. I must go now. They didn't give me much time. But remember what you have heard from Herod the Great.

Appendix 5

The following text is a first-person message by Alice Mathews. Mathews is the Lois W. Bennett Distinguished Professor of Educational Ministries and Women's Ministries at Gordon-Conwell Seminary in South Hamilton, Massachusetts, and cohost of *Discover the Word,* a daily radio program heard across the United States. This presentation was originally written for a *Discover the Word* radio program aired in November of 1991.

Sermon Idea: Only fools leave God out of their lives.

Subject: What is the danger of leaving God out of our lives?

Complement: Everything in our lives comes to nothing.

Purpose: For listeners to understand how important it is to build their lives and their plans around God.

Stance: The contemporary audience is transported back to the first century to hear the testimony of Joanna, the rich fool's wife.

Simon Said

Luke 12:15–21

The first time Simon brought up the subject at the dinner table, I thought he was kidding. Here we were on this huge farm, and he was talking about tearing down all the barns and building bigger ones in their place. I wondered what in the world we wanted more barns for. We couldn't use up in a year all the grain we had stored in the barns we already had.

But Simon kept talking about it. He said, "Look, Joanna, suppose we have famine next year or the year after? Then what? We'll lose everything we have. We'll starve to death. Our children will starve. We have to make provision for the future. It's foolish not to do so."

I couldn't think of any good reasons not to do what he wanted to do. But something inside me wasn't comfortable. It was true that we had one of the most successful farms in the country. It seemed that whatever Simon planted grew. He always seemed to get more grain from each plant than any of the other farmers in the district.

Yet another part of me kept thinking that there were other things we could do with all the produce and grain. I had seen some of the poor gleaners in our fields after the harvest. I knew that we could give them bags of grain and never miss them. It didn't seem necessary to keep all of it for ourselves.

Or we could sell more grain in the market and give the money to God. Somehow, we had so much, it seemed that we could do more than give God a tithe of this and a tithe of that.

But I couldn't put these ideas into words for Simon. He would just scoff at me as a foolish old woman trying to give away all his hard-earned wealth. He couldn't tolerate what he thought was nonsense. And I knew he'd think I was being stupid.

That winter, with our barns bulging with another bumper crop, Simon began meeting every week with an architect and a builder. They pored over sketches. They walked back and forth over the land. They had one purpose—to build the most space possible for the money. Meanwhile, we used so little of what was already in the barns, I became more and more convinced than ever that this was a foolish venture.

As we approached the Passover, the builders arrived and began driving their stakes into the ground. Day by day I watched walls go up, joined by joists and rafters. Roofs went on. As one new barn was finished, the old barn was emptied into it and torn down to make room for the next new barn. I couldn't believe how quickly the work moved forward.

Of course, Simon wanted it that way. He was always a man of decision. When he made up his mind how things would be, nothing ever got in his way. He just pushed ahead without thought for God or man. He used to say to me, "Joanna, anybody who plans well, ends well. It's all in the planning. If you do your homework, you can get anything you want."

His goal was to have all the new barns finished before harvest began. I could tell that he was going to meet his goal. But then, Simon always met his goals. The last new barn was finished just as harvest began. Just as Simon said it would be.

I have to say it was a good feeling to look out at the barns and see them strong and solid in the sunshine. I began to think that Simon had been right all along. It gives a person a nice secure feeling to have so much stored away for a rainy day.

But then I'd look out at some of those gleaners. Some were old women, bent double, trying to find a few grains of wheat here, a few there, that the harvesters had left behind. I saw small children crawling along the ground, looking for something they could take home for a meal. I kept asking myself, is it right to have so much when others have so little? Perhaps I could persuade Simon to give some of our food away.

When I brought up the subject at supper that night, I wasn't prepared for his reaction. He practically screamed at me: "Woman, you don't know what you're talking about! Do you think I worked hard for all that just to feed somebody else? Don't be crazy! That's MINE! It doesn't belong to anyone else. Do you hear? It's MINE! I earned it and I'll keep it." I knew then that I could never say anything that would change his mind.

One night shortly after that bad scene, everything changed. Simon had eaten well and was in an expansive mood. My brothers had come to visit, and after supper Simon had taken them on a tour of the new barns. Later the men were sitting around on the roof of our house in the cool evening. I heard Simon talking. He was saying, "You asked me how I managed to get so much stored away in these new barns. There's just one answer: planning. If you plan right, you can do anything you want to do. That's all it takes. Now I've got enough stored in my barns to last me many years. I'm thinking seriously of retiring, of taking my ease. Eat, drink, and be merry! That's what I'm going to do! You plan well and work hard, and it all comes back to you. You can retire when you want to and live out a full life in comfort."

I was a bit nervous when I heard him say that. Simon's words had alarmed me, just as I said. He had never told me he was building bigger barns just so he could "eat, drink, and be merry." So I found I was uneasy all evening. Eventually my brothers left and Simon got ready for bed.

He seemed so satisfied with himself. He knew he was the richest farmer in our entire district. I have to say he had worked hard for all he had gotten. But it didn't sound right, somehow, the way he bragged about all he had. It was as if God hadn't sent the rain at the right time and sunshine in abundance to make the crops grow. I kept thinking of all the bad things that could have happened—grasshoppers or drought or hail. Any of those could have wiped out the entire crop. But when Simon talked, it was as if he were taking credit for his wealth and he didn't have God to thank at all.

When we went to bed that night, Simon seemed to go off to sleep right away. I lay there thinking about the things he had said, worrying about them, I guess. I reached over to pull the blanket up over his shoulder. He didn't move. For some reason that surprised me. I raised up on one elbow and leaned over to touch him. He still didn't move. I couldn't hear him breathing. I leaned closer, not sure why I was doing that. Then I realized that he wasn't breathing.

I dashed off to find one of the servants. By the time we got back, we could tell that Simon was dead. Dead! I knew why I had been so uneasy about building all those new barns and why I was so worried when I heard Simon bragging to my brothers about his wealth.

All this happened three years ago. Of course, we had a large funeral the next day. Then the bickering over the farm began. In the end Simon's brother got all of it since we had no sons. It hasn't been easy, watching him sell off parts of the farm and put the money into some bad investments.

Three years have passed. One day in the marketplace I heard a new rabbi preach. They said his name was Jesus. A group of us who went to hear him each time he passed through our village have continued to meet together each week to talk about his teachings and the way he has changed our lives.

This evening my daughters and I went to the meeting. Our leader read us a letter from the half-brother of our rabbi, a man named James. It was a wonderful letter! But toward the end of it James said some things that made me think of Simon again. James wrote, "Now listen, you who say, 'Today or tomorrow we will go to this or that city, spend a year there, carry on business and make money.' Why, you don't even know what will happen tomorrow. What is your life? You are a mist that appears for a little while and then vanishes. Instead, you ought to say, 'If it is the Lord's will, we will live and do this or that.' As it is, you boast and brag. All such boasting is evil. Anyone, then, who knows the good he ought to do and doesn't do it, sins."

I sat there wondering, would it have made any difference at all if Simon had heard that? Would Simon have lived differently if he had known that we can't leave God out of our planning? Would anything have been different? I wonder.

Appendix 6

The following is a sermon by Torrey Robinson, written for his wife, Sue, to portray. Torrey Robinson currently pastors the First Baptist Church in Tarrytown, New York. The text that follows is the manuscript of the message originally presented by Sue Robinson on Easter, 1993.

Sermon Idea: Jesus is alive, so go spread the good news!

Subject: How can you know that Jesus is alive?

Complement: Because Mary Magdalene saw him, talked to him, and touched him.

Purpose: To present the gospel to nonbelievers in a compelling way and to challenge believers to share the good news.

Stance: The contemporary audience is transported back to the first century, a few weeks after the resurrection. They become the ancient audience—followers of Jesus in Galilee with whom Mary Magdalene shares her testimony concerning Christ's resurrection.

No Reason to Cry

John 20:1–18

I know you were expecting to meet with Peter, and I am aware you have already received word of Jesus' crucifixion. I too have known the grief you feel and that is why I am here.

[*Closing her eyes and taking a deep breath*]

I do so enjoy it here outside Tiberias on the shore of Galilee—the fresh air, a gentle breeze off the sea. It is so quiet and peaceful. You don't have to fight the crowds like they do in Jerusalem.

The news Peter has sent me to tell you sounds too good to be true. In fact, I'm afraid if I just come right out and tell you, you might not believe what I have to say. So allow me to tell you something about myself before I tell you why I'm here.

I suppose I should begin by introducing myself: my name is Mary. I know some of you already. Though I doubt many of you remember who I am, I suspect most of you will remember who I was. You see I grew up close by in Magdala.

I can see in some of your eyes a hint of recognition. And you are right. It is I. Mad Mary some people called me, or Mary Queen of Kooks. But I assure you I was never insane. I was tormented, possessed by seven demons.

Some of you lived in fear of me, but it was I who was terrorized. Day after day the never-ending pain took the sunshine from my sky. Night after night brought nothing more than a sleepless craving for the dawn. Alone, rejected by family and friends, my only company was the demons who tormented me.

Often I thought of suicide. "What is the good of such a painful existence?" I wondered. "Life is for those who can greet it with a smile. The sunshine is for those who can open eyes and heart to welcome its radiance. Life is good for the fit and active; but what has it to give to those like me whose mind and body have been imprisoned by invisible bars?"

Each day I sank deeper and deeper into my depression, retiring further and further within myself until . . . I heard him speak my name. "Mary," he said, as if waking me from a deep slumber. "Mary," I heard the sound of a wonderful voice. Someone was speaking my name. "I have driven the demons away," he said.

Freedom! Release from my pain! When no one else could help. When very few even cared to help, Jesus delivered me from my demonic possession.

That was the moment when the cloud lifted from my mind, when my body felt again the power of rich strong life coursing through my veins. It was a moment I'll never forget.

The days following brought back no return of my trouble. Each morning I arose to greet the new day, at first with a faint concern as to whether the cure was indeed complete. But such wonder soon passed. I was whole again. Now the sunshine seemed to greet me with its warm smile. Now I heard the birds singing, and they seemed to sing to me. The Master had given me life again.

It was then that I determined to follow him. Others had followed Jesus, but none had better motivation than I had. He had given me back my life; perhaps I could use that life to minister in some small way to him.

I served the Master for the past two years. As you know, I was not alone. There were many other women who followed Jesus. I developed special friendships with two women, Joanna who married Cuza, manager of Herod's household, and of course Susanna. She is such a generous woman. These were women, like myself, who pledged themselves to support Jesus' ministry, any way possible.

At first, I was unsure how I could be of any service to him.

But almost immediately I realized that I could help out in a very practical way. Jesus and the disciples needed financial support. After all, the Master did not come from a wealthy family. He was a carpenter's son. Jesus had little money. And of the twelve disciples, only the tax collector, Matthew, had much money before joining their ranks.

So, many women committed ourselves to give what we had to help meet the financial needs of Jesus' ministry. I don't think they could have kept the ministry going without our sacrifices. But I can honestly say they were sacrifices from loving hearts.

Another thing I soon realized: Jesus, and particularly his disciples, needed to have a woman around. I helped with the cooking and some of you know how Peter can eat. I remember one time on the other side of the Sea of Galilee, perhaps some of you were there, Jesus had to feed five thousand men plus their wives and children, and all he had were five loaves of bread and two fish. He gave the food to his disciples to pass out to the crowd. I remember thinking: it will take quite a miracle to feed all these thousands of people. The real miracle was to feed the disciples, the other ten thousand people or so were "a piece of cake," so to speak.

So I took care of some of the food for Jesus and his disciples and I helped make arrangements for their hospitality in various towns. They always seemed to have more important things on their minds, but I ask you, what can be more important than eating a good breakfast and getting a good night's sleep?

These were all only small sacrifices made from a grateful heart. I would have done anything for Jesus. Not only had he met my deepest need, I saw in him the capacity to do the same for others. Jesus was a man of incredible powers. He healed men and women of lifelong and life-threatening diseases. He made the lame to walk and the blind to see. As in my life, when he spoke, even the demons obeyed. People came from miles around to see him, to hear him, to touch him. There was a growing sense of excitement about the Master and the kingdom he talked so much about.

And one day, only a few weeks ago, as Jesus entered Jerusalem, the excitement reached an all-time high. People lined the streets to see Jesus. The crowds cheered. Some waved palm branches. Many were shouting things like "Hosanna!" and "Blessed is he who comes in the name of the Lord!" Those of us with Jesus joined in the celebration, singing and dancing, joining in the cheers. We were sure that this was the time we had anticipated and talked about for many months. There were whispers that during the Passover celebration Jesus would offer himself to the Jewish people as their king. Our jubilation was unbounded.

But then it all came crashing down. Almost overnight the mood changed. The joy, the celebration and singing gave way to anxiety, weeping, and fear. Somehow I had sensed it before. I had sensed a somberness in Jesus even in the celebration. I had seen it reflected in his eyes from the time he determined to return to Jerusalem, but I did not believe it or at least I refused to accept it.

On Thursday night, with the cheers and the singing of the preceding days still ringing in my ears, I heard the news that Jesus had been arrested. I watched at a distance as they took him to be executed. The Jewish leaders had been plotting this quietly for months, but there was one small thing that stood in their way—justice. On trumped-up charges they accused him of treason and blasphemy.

They led him before the Jewish and Roman authorities in a mockery of justice.

It wasn't terribly surprising that the Jewish leaders would believe the charges, for their disdain for Jesus was no secret. As we discovered later, the bogus charges were their idea in the first place. Blatant lies by disreputable witnesses were hastily accepted without question. At first, I wondered why the Master didn't speak in his defense, but then I realized that the Jews weren't looking for guilt or innocence, only an excuse to do away with him.

But I expected better from the Romans. Surely Jesus could plead his case before a Roman court. Surely they would see through this sham. But it was Roman guards who put a robe on his back and a crown made from thorns on his head. It was they who mocked him, scourged him, and spat upon him. It was Roman governors, Herod, and Pilate who refused to do what justice demanded. It was they who bowed to the pressure from the Jews. It was Romans who turned Jesus over to the crowd to be crucified.

I stood there as they nailed him to a cross. I do not know which was worse, the murderers with whom he was crucified or the murderers who crucified him. It all happened so fast. I did not know what to do. I did not know what to think.

I had watched this same man heal the sick and the lame. I had seen him perform great miracles. From my own experience I knew the power he had to cast out demons. And I never doubted the disciples' claim that even the wind and the sea obeyed his commands. He had the very power of God at his disposal. Deep down, in my horror at the cruelty done to him, I believed he would not die. If, in fact, he was God's Son, I reasoned, he could not die.

As he hung up on that cross, I expected, at any moment that Jesus would come down from the cross. When the soldiers mockingly challenged him to save himself, I fully expected that he would. When they nailed him to that tree, my hopes, my dreams, my security were all nailed up there with him. Jesus was the one who had delivered me from my demonic tormentors. He was the one who had given me reason to live. I had pledged my life to Jesus. He simply couldn't die . . . but he did.

To that point, as I watched Jesus suffer in agony on the cross, I shed few tears. Until he drew his last breath, I reasoned that while there was life, there was hope. But when his head dropped in death, a part of me died too. When his suffering had ended, mine had only begun.

I walked with them as they placed his lifeless body in the tomb. With night falling and the Sabbath approaching, our time at the tomb was limited, but I hated to leave the tomb. I had no place else to go and nothing more to live for.

There was no rest for me that Sabbath. There was no worship for me on that holy day either. Too many dark questions shrouded my view of God. Why did this happen? Why didn't Jesus save himself? Did he really have power over Satan and death or was it all an illusion? What did this mean for the world? What did this mean for me?

Oh, how the hours of that Sabbath dragged. As exhausted as I was that night, I could not sleep. I sat. I stood. I paced back and forth. I anxiously awaited the dawn and finally, while it was still dark, at the first hint of morning's light, I set out for the tomb in Joseph's garden.

It was too dark to see inside the tomb, but not too dark to see that the stone that had been put there to seal the tomb had been rolled away. I wondered who could have moved the stone. All I could think was that someone had taken the body.

In bewilderment and fear, I ran to tell the disciples. Breathlessly, I explained what I had seen to Peter and John who quickly left me to examine the scene for themselves.

By the time I returned to the tomb, Peter and John were gone. I had hoped that they could help me figure out what had happened to my Master's body, to help me find out who had taken it. I was more confused and dejected than ever. I did not know what to do. I was not sure what to think. All the strain of the last days burst out like a flood. Grief-stricken, exhausted, bewildered, overwhelmed, I could not hold back the tears.

[*Addressing her audience directly*]

But I am not here to tell you news of Christ's death. You already know about that. This is going to be hard to believe, but I'm here to tell you, Jesus is alive.

[*Pausing . . .*]

Oh, I can see it in your eyes, you don't believe me. I can understand. I couldn't believe it either, at first. I did not believe easily. I faced my grief honestly.

I looked into the tomb; there were two men inside. In my grief and tears, I really never did get a good look at either of them. I remember they asked me why I was crying.

"What a stupid question!" I thought at first. They were in the tomb. They must have known what had happened. Everyone else in Jerusalem knew about it. How could anyone ask such a question when everything I had longed for, everything I had hoped for, everything I had trusted in was gone?

I wondered if perhaps they had taken the body. "They have taken my Lord away, and I don't know where they have put him," was all I could say.

Having found no comfort in that conversation, I turned to leave, my eyes still clouded with tears. There behind me was another man who I assumed to be the caretaker of the garden. Seeing my tears, he too asked me why I was crying.

"Doesn't anyone understand?" I thought to myself. "Doesn't anyone know my loneliness, my heartache, my fear?"

With one word I realized someone did understand. All he said was "Mary," and I believed the impossible. Once before, when I was held captive by demonic powers, that voice had spoken my name and I had been set free. Now, with the mention of my name, Jesus broke through my pain and grief and touched my soul.

I fell down before him in wonder, amazement, and joy and cried out, "Rabboni! Teacher!" I clutched his ankles and never wanted to let go. He just said to me gently, "Do not hold on to me, for I have yet to return to my Father. Go instead to my brothers and tell them I am returning to my Father and your Father, my God and your God."

And that is why Peter sent me to talk with you. So you could know that *Jesus is not dead—he lives! I know it sounds impossible, but I have seen him. I have talked to him. I have touched him. Jesus is alive!* Jesus in the greatest of miracles has conquered death.

We're just beginning to understand why all of this had to happen. But his death was for me. It was for you, so that through his resurrection you can have new life and a new relationship with God. If only you will believe and follow him.

And that is the message he has left us to tell the world. I am trying to tell as many people as I can. *Tell everyone, "Jesus is alive!"* And if we're faithful in sharing this wonderful news, in days and years to come, in places we cannot even imagine, they too will respond to this great news of hope and be set free.

Appendix 7

The following is another sermon by Torrey Robinson, pastor of the First Baptist Church in Tarrytown, New York. The text that follows is the manuscript of a sermon originally preached in his church on Easter Sunday, 2000.

Sermon Idea: The gospel, the good news, is always and only the great news of God's grace in Jesus Christ.

Subject: How can Paul be so sure of his message of the gospel of grace?

Complement: Because it was this message, passed on to him from Jesus Christ himself, that transformed Paul's life.

Purpose: The purpose of this sermon was shaped by the fact that it was preached on Easter Sunday as a first sermon in a series from Galatians.

1. To share the gospel by challenging those who trust their own works to see that their salvation is dependent upon Jesus alone.
2. To introduce the Book of Galatians.

Stance: Paul is transported to the twenty-first century to talk to the congregation at First Baptist about his letter.

God's Good News

Galatians 1:1–2:10

[*Speaker takes off his suit coat and puts on a sleeveless robe and begins in character as the apostle Paul*]

I am pleased that your pastor has seen the significance of the letter I, Paul, wrote to the Galatian churches almost two thousand years ago. I understand that he plans to study it together with you in the coming weeks. So many years have passed since I wrote that letter, I'm afraid it may seem irrelevant to some of you. Yet even today, it is a letter that has something to say to those who have been Christians for a long time as well as those who are still on the way.

Some of you may not know what caused me to write this letter. I wrote out of concern for the churches that I had started on my first missionary journey. On that first trip I and two companions, Barnabas and John Mark, traveled to Cyprus and then on to Galatia. I believe you are familiar with Cyprus, that island in the eastern Mediterranean Sea, but the area of Galatia today has a different name. I believe you know it as southeastern Turkey.

That was the itinerary of my first missionary journey, across Cyprus and on to Galatia. Some of the cities we visited were Pisidian Antioch, Iconium, Lystra, and Derbe. But having visited these cities and started churches there, I had a great interest in how the churches were doing in my absence. Some time later I heard news from the Christians there that a sad thing had happened. Apparently, some people had come into their fellowship and began to undermine the foundation I had laid in those churches. They were teaching that a relationship with God really boiled down to a list of do's and don'ts. Such teaching ignored the fundamental of God's grace. Anyway, when I heard about that, my first impulse was to travel back and straighten the matter out myself, but I could not do that. Instead, I wrote a letter, the letter you have in your Bibles that you call Galatians.

All that is to tell you, this letter is important to me; nevertheless I seldom visit churches just to introduce my letters. While I'm honored that your pastor invited me to come, I have to tell you, if it weren't for the importance of this day, if it weren't for the significance of the resurrection of Jesus Christ, I wouldn't be here this morning. But the message of Easter and the message of my letter to the Galatians share a great deal in common. Let me see if I can explain as I introduce my letter to the Galatians to you.

Though I haven't met you personally, I know something about you. I know how you are tempted when you pick up one of my letters to skip over the introductory material and get right to the meat of it. But in this letter especially, from the outset I wanted those who read this letter to understand something very important. That's why I begin, "Paul, an apostle." Don't let anyone tell you that God doesn't have a sense of humor. He called me to be an apostle. Now I know what some of you may be thinking: how can Paul be an apostle because he certainly wasn't one of the Twelve. And you're absolutely right. In fact, there was a time when I opposed everything the apostles stood for. Or should I say, they opposed everything that I stood for.

Let me tell you what I stood for:

1. I believed and I taught at one time that the Jews are God's chosen people. His only people. If anyone wanted to have a relationship with God, he or she had to become a Jew.
2. I believed that if you hoped to have a relationship with the Holy God, you had to live a righteous life. How else could a righteous God accept you?
3. I opposed Jesus and his followers because they caused people to deny that keeping all the Jewish laws was essential to earn God's favor.
4. If sincerity counts in your evaluation of me, I want you to know that I was sincere, to the point of persecuting those who followed Jesus. I took delight in destroying the church and especially in causing men and women to denounce their faith in Jesus.

Yet despite all that, I stand before you today as an apostle, not because I pretend to have had any special relationship with Jesus before he died. The fact is, like most Pharisees, I hated him and I was glad that he died. Nevertheless, despite that fact, Jesus sought me out after he died. I am an eyewitness to his resurrection, for even as I was on my way to destroy his church in Damascus, the risen Lord appeared to me. The resurrected Lord commissioned me himself to proclaim the good news, not primarily to the Jews, but to the Gentiles. As I said, you can't tell me God doesn't have a sense of humor.

So it is significant when I wrote, "Grace and peace to you from God our Father and the Lord Jesus Christ, who gave himself for our sins to rescue us from the present evil age, according to the will of our God and Father, to whom be glory for ever and ever. Amen" (Gal. 1:3–5).

Grace. Now that's a word that is loaded with significance. In fact, this letter which some of you have open before you this morning is all about grace. I wanted to come today, before your pastor began a study of my letter to the Galatians, to tell you how important this letter is. It was important when I first wrote the letter to the churches I had visited on my first missionary journey, and it is still important to you today because grace is so easy for all of us to lose hold of.

Grace and Peace. God commissioned me, a Hebrew of Hebrews, to be an ambassador to the Gentiles. The Jewish system with which I was raised, the Pharisaical system I espoused, shut you Gentiles out. Oh, God has always made a way for those who truly believed in him, but if you wanted to know God, you had to become a Jew. If you were a male, you had to be circumcised. Male or female, you had to submit to the Jewish law. God provided a way, but he was much more accepting of Gentiles than most of us Jews were.

Along with many of my kinsmen, I arrogantly believed in the idea that we, the Jews, were the chosen people. Technically, I know that is true, but I took it to mean that God cared for Jews and only Jews. Some of us could say the most terrible things—"God loves only Israel of all the nations he has made"; "God will judge Israel with one measure and the Gentiles with another"; "The best of the snakes crush; the best of the Gentiles kill"; "God created the Gentiles to be fuel for the fires of hell." We even had a law that made it illegal to help a Gentile mother in her sorest hour of labor pain, for that would only bring another Gentile into the world.

In Jesus, the Messiah, both Jews and Gentiles have equal access to God. In Jesus, the religious system that created hostility between Jews and Gentiles was broken down. In him, Jews and Gentiles can find peace with God and, because of that, can have peace with one another.

Yet what distressed me when I wrote my letter to the Galatians and what distresses me still today is how people can take the good news of Jesus and distort it. They can take God's message of grace and peace and remove the grace and so destroy the peace. What some proclaim as gospel, or good news, is in fact, bad news. They maintain that a relationship with God is based on a standard before which we all fall short. From my day to yours, I have found that people pervert the grace of God and try to establish a relationship with God based on their religious works rather than upon Jesus' work on the cross.

I must tell you, I have absolutely no tolerance for such people, whether they are Jewish or Christian, Catholic or Baptist. I understand that you live in a culture of tolerance. In many ways tolerating differences is a good thing. Christians, more than anyone else, should be models of how to deal with cultural, ethnic, and political differences. Yet when it comes to the truth, tolerance is deadly. When a house is burning, you can't tolerate those who remain in bed believing that the flames will not hurt them. Differences of opinion can be tolerated, but untruth cannot, for it can harm or even destroy people.

So it is with the message of God's grace. It is the best news known to anyone that God sent his Son, Jesus, to die for your sins and mine. It is certainly good news that on the cross, that day you call Good Friday, Jesus paid the penalty our sins deserve. That is the message of God's grace. Jesus paid it all. Salvation cannot be earned, no matter how hard we try. It is simply a gift we receive by faith.

But unfortunately, in my time and yours, many speak of good news, but have nothing good to say. Even today, on Resurrection Sunday, many religious leaders will speak of the gospel from their pulpits, but what they proclaim is no gospel at all. Make no mistake; it doesn't matter whether the one who proclaims it calls himself pastor, father, priest, or rabbi. Even if the pastor of this church or an angel from heaven should preach a gospel other than the gospel of grace about which I have spoken, let him be damned! I cannot say it too strongly. If anybody is preaching to you a gospel other than what you accepted, let him be damned! For that is precisely what such a false gospel does to those who hear it and embrace it.

I know such inflammatory statements are not popular in your day, nor were they in my own. Unfortunately, there are those who say what people want to hear. And many people have a hard time hearing that God gives salvation as a gift. If they can't earn it, they don't seem to want it. Such people take the good news of Jesus, the gospel of grace, and turn it back into a religion, a rule-keeping system.

But you ask me, how can I be so sure that I am right? How do I know that the good news I proclaim is in fact the truth?

As I told you, I am an apostle, not because I was called as one of Jesus' followers before he died; rather I was called as one of Jesus' followers after he died and rose again. Many in my day would dispute with me that I could be an apostle for I had not been a witness to the resurrection, but I can report that in fact I was. A great light blinded me. Yet in my blindness I saw clearly for the first time, for it was Jesus who appeared to me on the road to Damascus. It was he who gave me the gospel, the great news of God's grace through his sacrificial death on a Roman cross. No man taught me this good news but Jesus himself. I received it in a revelation from the risen Lord.

And anyone who knew who I was and what I was like will attest that something changed me, something radically changed me. My life was turned upside down. God's call on my life was so ironic; it was funny. For I, who before all who knew me lived a blameless life, discovered that all the time I had been fighting against God. I, Paul, who had set out to destroy the church, was commissioned to plant and build it. I, perhaps the most zealous of all Jews, was called by God's grace as an apostle to minister to the Gentiles.

The gospel, the good news that had been entrusted to me for the Gentiles, had been given to me straight from Jesus himself, no one else. True, he sent me to Ananias in Damascus to be baptized, and I spent time in the area around Damascus referred to as Arabia. I began to minister in Damascus, and I, who had persecuted Christians, became the target of an assassination plot by my own people, the Jews.

But I didn't go up to Jerusalem for three years. Finally, after three years, I made my way to Jerusalem and stayed with Peter for fifteen days. During that time the only other apostle I spoke to was James, the Lord's brother. Later, I went back to the area where I grew up in Syria and Cilicia. But the churches in Judea had no influence on the gospel I proclaimed. All they knew was that the man who once persecuted the church had been tamed by the fiery love of Christ. The one who once tried to destroy the faith was now preaching it.

Finally, fourteen years later, I went back to Jerusalem; this time I went back with Barnabas and Titus. I had another revelation from God that directed me to meet with the leaders of Jerusalem to share with them the good news I preach to the Gentiles. I wanted to make sure that after all these years of preaching and serving God I had gotten it right, and they agreed with me that I had. They agreed that the gospel, the good news, is always and only the great news of God's grace in Jesus Christ. It doesn't involve keeping religious rules but only to believe that Jesus died for our sins.

The apostles agreed that God's hand was upon me to preach to the Gentiles, just as he had called Peter to preach to the Jews. They welcomed Barnabas, Titus, and me into their fellowship as fellow believers and leaders. They added nothing to our message. They only encouraged us as we went to minister to the Gentile churches not to forget the financially struggling Christians in Jerusalem. That was certainly something I was happy to do.

I am so committed to this gospel of grace; I have to tell you that I even confronted Peter when I saw that he was practicing a double standard in the church in Antioch. You see there was a time when Peter too had received a revelation from God about the Gentiles, and he too was unafraid to eat with them. But certain men in the Jerusalem church came up to Antioch and began to exert their influence on him so that he no longer ate with the Gentiles who would eat nonkosher foods. Behind this practice was the belief that you could not be a Christian if you didn't keep all the Jewish laws. This form of religious rule keeping was contrary to grace.

It didn't matter who the person was. Wrong teaching had to be confronted publicly. The gospel isn't about religion or going to church or even how often you read your Bible and pray, as important as those things are. The gospel, the good news, is always and only the great news of God's grace in Jesus Christ. So, since Peter was a leader and his influence had a significant effect on everyone, I rebuked him openly, to set him and the church straight.

You ask me why I feel so strongly about this; the answer is no doubt wrapped up in who I was and who I am. The reality of the resurrection changed me from an enemy of Jesus to an ambassador of his grace. God enabled me to see myself not as the one who looks the best on the outside. I began to see what I was really like on the inside. God saved me when I was out to destroy his work. He brought me to himself when I was on my way to persecute and arrest Christians in Damascus. God called me to himself when I, in my zeal, was his enemy. If it weren't for God's grace, his unmerited favor, I would have died an enemy of Jesus, never an ambassador for him.

I proclaim to you here today, Jesus Christ is alive from the dead. I know. I have seen him. He has spoken to me. Do you know what the resurrected Messiah's first words were to me? "Saul, Saul, why do you persecute me?" I was fighting the very God I professed to serve. My zeal for my religious cause had actually made me God's enemy. I can tell you from experience that some of you who are the most devout in your religious commitment will be in for the biggest surprise. Like me, you may discover that what you thought to be righteous acts turn out to be a sort of futile self-deception.

Yet in his marvelous wit and his boundless grace, God appointed me, the zealous Jew, Saul of Tarsus, to be Paul the apostle of Jesus to the Gentiles—an ambassador of his grace. Today, Resurrection Sunday, is a day to rejoice, for Jesus is alive. Celebrate his life! Celebrate his grace!

[Speaker *steps back, takes off the robe, puts on the suit coat, and speaks to the congregation as pastor*]

What we have just heard from the apostle Paul in his letter to the Galatians calls for a response. Some of you have grown up hearing a different gospel. Yet today, perhaps for the first time you have heard the good news of God's grace through Jesus Christ. Let me make it as clear as I can. Imagine in your hand you hold all the good things you have been trusting in to make God pleased with you. Imagine God holding out his hand to you to offer you his grace. You cannot receive his grace until you let go of all the acts of self-effort that are in your hands.

Today, listen to the testimony of the apostle Paul. If anyone could have made it on his self-righteousness, it was he, but it doesn't work that way because none of us is good enough. Today, perhaps God has pursued you to this place. Perhaps like Paul you were on your way to do your thing, but God has broken through to you. You need to respond.

A man stood on the edge of a towering cliff. As he looked to the jagged rocks below, he realized that to fall would mean almost certain death. Yet even as he contemplated the thought, the ground gave way beneath his feet, and he slid over the edge of the cliff.

The man reached out frantically for something to stop his slide, now a sheer fall to his death. He managed to grab hold of a small tree growing out of the side of the cliff, and he cried out to God for help.

The next second there was hovering over him an angel sent from God. The man continued to cling to the tiny tree as he looked up at the angel.

"Do you believe I can save you?" the angel asked.

The man looked at the angel's strong arms and mighty wings and replied, "Yes! I do believe you can save me."

The angel questioned the man again: "Do you believe I will save you?"

The man's grip on the tree was beginning to weaken as he looked up at the caring smile and tender eyes of the angel. He responded, "Yes! Yes, I believe you will save me."

The angel said, "Then let go."

Perhaps you are here this morning, clinging to your goodness, hanging on to your own righteousness, trusting in your own efforts to be right with God. As you see yourself before God this morning clinging to those things, he has two words to say to you: "Let go."

Appendix 8

Bibliography of Resources for the First-Person Preacher

Recommended First-Person Preaching Resources

For Extra-Biblical Research on Biblical Characters

Barclay, William. *The Master's Men*. Nashville: Abingdon, 1969.

Brownrigg, Ronald. *Who's Who in the New Testament*. New York: Holt, Rinehart & Winston, 1971.

Buechner, Frederick. *Peculiar Treasures: A Biblical Who's Who*. San Francisco: Harper and Row, 1979.

Comay, Joan. *Who's Who in the Old Testament*. New York: Holt, Rinehart & Winston, 1971.

Deen, Edith. *All the Women of the Bible*. New York: Harper and Brothers, 1955.

Harrison, Everett F. *Jesus and His Contemporaries*. Grand Rapids: Baker, 1970.

Hercus, John. *David*. Chicago: InterVarsity, 1968.

———. *More Pages from God's Case-Book: Isaiah and the Assyrians, Jeremiah, Ezekiel*. 2nd ed. Carlisle, England: Solway, 1996.

———. *Pages from God's Case-Book: Pharaoh, Nebuchadnezzar, Saul, Joseph*. 3rd ed. Carlisle, England: Solway, 1996.

Macartney, Clarence. *Chariots of Fire and Other Sermons on Old Testament Heroes*. Nashville: Cokesbury, 1935.

Speakman, Frederick. *Love Is Something You Do*. Old Tappan, N.J.: Fleming Revell, 1959.

Steinsaltz, Adin. *Biblical Images*. New York: Basic, 1984.

Weatherhead, Leslie. *Personalities of the Passion*. Nashville: Abingdon, 1943.

Whyte, Alexander. *Bible Characters*. Grand Rapids: Zondervan, 1968.

Wiesel, Elie. *Five Biblical Portraits*. London: University of Notre Dame Press, 1981.

———. *Messengers of God*. New York: Random House, 1976.

Wright, G. Ernest, ed. *Great People of the Bible and How They Lived*. New York: Reader's Digest, 1979.

Researching the Historical Setting

Works of Historical Fiction

Frank Slaughter has been one of the most prolific writers in this category, with works too numerous to list.

Douglas, Lloyd C. *The Robe*. Boston: Houghton-Mifflin, 1969.

Ourslcr, Fulton. *The Greatest Faith Ever Known*. New York: Doubleday, 1953.

Historical Studies

Bammel, Ernst, and C. F. D. Moule, eds. *Jesus and the Politics of His Day*. New York: Cambridge University Press, 1985.

Beers, V. Gilbert. *The Victor Handbook of Bible Knowledge*. Wheaton: Victor, 1984.

Blaiklock, E. M. *The Archaeology of the New Testament*. Nashville: Thomas Nelson, 1984.

Bruce, F. F. *New Testament History*. New York: Doubleday Anchor, 1972.

Coleman, William L. *Today's Handbook of Bible Times and Customs*. Minneapolis: Bethany House, 1984.

Edersheim, Alfred. *The History of the Jewish Nation*. 3d ed. Grand Rapids: Baker, 1979.

Frank, Harry Thomas, ed. *Atlas of the Bible*. 4th ed. New York: Reader's Digest, 1987.

Jeremias, Joachim. *Jerusalem in the Time of Jesus*. 3d ed. Philadelphia: Fortress, 1978.

Meeks, Wayne A. *The Moral World of the First Christians*. Philadelphia: Westminster, 1986.

Severy, Merle, ed. *Everyday Life in Bible Times, 4th Century* B.C. Washington, D.C.: National Geographic, 1968.

Stambaugh, John, and David Balch. *The New Testament in Its Social Environment*. Philadelphia: Westminister, 1986.

Resources for Your First-Person Presentation

Acting Resources

Blunt, Jerry. *More Stage Dialects*. New York: Harper and Row, 1980.

———. *Stage Dialects*. Scranton, Pa.: Chandler, 1966.

Cole, Toby, and Helen Krinch Chinoy, eds. *Actors on Acting*. New York: Crown Trade Paperbacks, 1970.

Moore, Sonia. *The Stanislavski System: The Professional Training of an Actor*. New York: Penguin, 1984.

Costume and Makeup

Corson, Richard. *Stage Makeup*. 6th ed. Englewood Cliffs, N.J.: Prentice-Hall, 1981.

Holt, Michael. *Costume and Make-up*. Schirmer Books Theatre Manuals Series. Edited by David Mayer. New York: Schirmer, 1988.

Notes

Key Terms

1. Harold Freeman, *Variety in Biblical Preaching* (Waco: Word, 1987), 26.

Chapter 2: Preaching As Listeners Like It

1. Freeman, *Biblical Preaching,* 26.

2. Helpful instruction on the power of story in preaching can be found in a recorded lecture series by Fred Craddock given at Western Seminary in Milwaukee, Oregon, 1986.

3. Fred Craddock, *As One Without Authority* (Enid, Okla.: The Phillips University Press, 1974), 78.

4. For an example, see the sermon in Appendix 7.

Chapter 3: Study! Study! Study!

1. J. H. Jowett, "The Preacher: His Life and Work," *The 1912 Yale Lectures* (New York: G. H. Doran, 1912), 113–14.

2. For an example, see the sermon in Appendix 6.

3. Elizabeth Achtemeier, *Creative Preaching: Finding the Words* (Nashville: Abingdon, 1980), 81.

4. For an example, see the sermon in Appendix 7.

5. For an example, see the sermon in Appendix 1.

6. For an example, see the sermon in Appendix 3.

7. For help with this, see chapter 3 of Gordon Fee and Doug Stewart, *How to Read the Bible for All It's Worth: A Guide to Understanding the Bible* (Grand Rapids: Zondervan, 1993), 78–93.

8. Considering most first-person sermons are drawn from biblical narrative and not all preachers are familiar with how to exegete narrative material, here is a summary of the exegetical process for biblical narrative as laid out by Paul Borden:

a. Determine the design of the story—Raise questions about why the story is designed as it is. Divide the story into scenes.

b. List the characters and note the action—Who is the main character, the protagonist, antagonist, etc.? The living out of life is not announced but accomplished, sometimes successfully, sometimes unsuccessfully, in the conflict of the drama.

c. Examine the dialogue (or monologue)—The major method for developing characterization is through words spoken by characters. Note the dialogue to appear first in a story and that which is repeated.

d. List narrator statements—The narrator's statements provide insights into God's perspective in the story.

e. Discover the plot—Determine the events that intensify disequilibrium. Determine where reversal occurs. Establish how the story is resolved.

f. Look at the story's tone, rhetorical structures, and context—Determine the story's tone, how it is being told. Look at rhetorical structures, often an anomaly in the pattern or structure points to the major idea being developed in the story. Examine the context of stories surrounding this narrative.

g. Determine the story's emphasis—Write a summary sentence for each paragraph in narrative, then create a single descriptive title for the entire paragraph.

h. State the story's main idea—Sum up what the story is about (its subject) and what the story has to say about it (the story's complement).

For a more complete explanation see Paul Borden, "Is There Really One Big Idea in That Story?" in Keith Willhite and Scott M. Gibson, eds., *The Big Idea of Biblical Preaching: Connecting the Bible to People* (Grand Rapids: Baker, 1998), 67–80.

9. For a fuller treatment of how to identify and develop the central idea of a text, see Haddon Robinson, *Biblical Preaching: The Development and Delivery of Expository Messages,* 2d ed. (Grand Rapids: Baker, 2001), 33–50.

10. Consult the list of suggested resources in Appendix 8.

11. Ibid.

12. Excerpt from the sermon in Appendix 2.

13. Excerpt adapted from the sermon in Appendix 4.

14. Gary Inrig, *The Parables: Understanding What Jesus Meant* (Grand Rapids: Discovery House, 1991), 37–38.

15. Information gathered from John E. Stambaugh and David L. Balch, *The New Testament in Its Social Environment,* Library of Early Christianity, ed. Wayne A. Meeks (Philadelphia: Westminster, 1986).

16. F. Nigel Hepper, *Baker Encyclopedia of Bible Plants* (Grand Rapids: Baker, 1992), 111–12.

17. See the sermon by Steve Mathewson in Appendix 1.

18. Unpublished class notes, J. Kent Edwards, "How to Prepare a First-Person Sermon—Methodology," Gordon-Conwell Seminary.

Chapter 4: O Say Can You See?

1. For an example, see the sermon in Appendix 2.

2. Fredrick B. Speakman, "What Pilate Said One Midnight," *The Twentieth Century Pulpit* 1 (1978): 214–19.

3. In the sermon in Appendix 7 the apostle Paul refers back to his own experience with the risen Lord as he addresses a modern audience.

4. Excerpt from the conclusion of the sermon in Appendix 6.

Chapter 5: Bones and Flesh

1. For a fuller treatment of the process involved in formulating the homiletical idea and determining the sermon's purpose, see Robinson, *Biblical Preaching,* 101–3.

2. For a clear exposition of the Book of Ruth, see Robert L. Hubbard Jr., *The Book of Ruth: The New International Commentary on the Old Testament* (Grand Rapids: Eerdmans, 1988).

3. Freeman, *Biblical Preaching,* 61–62.

4. The sermon manuscript in Appendix 6 shows the basic structure of the story filled out with exegetical and historical details.

5. See chapter 6 for more information on the delivery of a first-person sermon.

6. Excerpt from Appendix 2.

7. For an example, see the introduction to the sermon in Appendix 6.

8. For an example, see the introduction to the sermon in Appendix 2.

9. A dramatic exception to this might be the play *Our Town,* by Thornton Wilder, in which the stage manager, who is the primary character in the play, comments on the action on stage.

Chapter 6: It's All in How You Tell It

1. Toby Cole and Helen Krinch Chinoy, eds., *Actors on Acting* (New York: Crown Trade, 1970), 21.

2. Flora Davis, "How to Read Body Language," in *Rhetoric of Nonverbal Communication: Readings,* ed. Haig A. Bosmajian (Glenview, Ill: Scott, Foresman, 1971).

3. Sonia Moore, *The Stanislavski System: The Professional Training of an Actor* (New York: Penguin, 1984), 23.

4. Reg Grant and John Reed, *Stories to Touch the Heart* (Wheaton: Victor, 1990), 68–69.

5. Judy E. Yordon, *Roles in Interpretation,* 5th ed. (Boston: McGraw Hill, 2002).

6. Jac and Miriam Striezheff Lewis, *Costume: The Performing Partner* (Colorado Springs: Meriwether, 1990), 59.

7. Ibid., 46.

8. Ibid., 64.

9. Richard Corson, *Stage Makeup,* 6th ed. (Englewood Cliffs, N.J.: Prentice Hall, 1981), 24.

10. See Corson, *Stage Makeup*. Among the worthwhile information in this book that may prove helpful, you'll find a step-by-step process for determining and applying the appropriate makeup. The chapter on mustaches, beards, hair, and wigs is especially valuable. In addition, one of the appendices of the book contains extensive sketches of hairstyles of men and women throughout history

which may prove helpful in portraying characters from biblical times as well as figures from church history.

Chapter 7: Curing First-Person Headaches

1. Fee and Stuart, *How to Read the Bible,* 78.

2. For example, in Alice Mathews's message in Appendix 5, even though the parable of the rich fool is fairly well known, Mathews's treatment of it is fresh. The tension of the sermon would be lost if the passage were read before this first-person account was preached.

3. Unpublished class notes, J. Kent Edwards, "How to Prepare a First-Person Sermon—Methodology," Gordon-Conwell Seminary, 3.

4. John Hercus, *Pages From God's Case-Book,* 2nd ed. (London: InterVarsity, 1969), 108.

Haddon W. Robinson, Ph.D., is the Harold John Ockenga Distinguished Professor of Preaching at Gordon-Conwell Theological Seminary in South Hamilton, Massachusetts. His book, *Biblical Preaching,* has sold more than 200,000 copies and has been used extensively in Bible colleges and seminaries since 1980.

Torrey W. Robinson, D.Min., has pastored churches in Wisconsin and New Jersey and is currently the senior pastor of First Baptist Church in Tarrytown, New York.